RUBY
IN A NUTSHELL

A Desktop Quick Reference

RUBY
IN A NUTSHELL

A Desktop Quick Reference

Yukihiro Matsumoto

with translated text by David L. Reynolds, Jr.

O'REILLY®

Beijing • Cambridge • Farnham • Köln • Paris • Sebastopol • Taipei • Tokyo

Ruby in a Nutshell

by Yukihiro Matsumoto

Copyright © 2002 O'Reilly Media, Inc. All rights reserved.
Printed in the United States of America.

Published by O'Reilly Media, Inc., 1005 Gravenstein Highway North, Sebastopol, CA 95472

O'Reilly Media, Inc. books may be purchased for educational, business, or sales promotional use. Online editions are also available for most titles (*safari.oreilly. com*). For more information contact our corporate/institutional sales department: (800) 998-9938 or *corporate@oreilly.com*.

With content from *Ruby Pocket Reference* (O'Reilly Japan) translated by David L. Reynolds, Jr.

Editor: Laura Lewin

Production Editor: Mary Anne Weeks Mayo

Cover Designer: Hanna Dyer

Interior Designer: Melanie Wang

Printing History:

January 2002:   First Edition.

 This book uses RepKover™, a durable and flexible lay-flat binding.

ISBN: 0-596-00214-9
[M]   [9/05]

Foreword

Ruby is an object-oriented programming language developed for the purpose of making programming both enjoyable and fast. With its easy-to-use interpreter, easy-to-understand syntax, complete object-oriented functionality, and powerful class libraries, Ruby has become a language that can be used in a broad range of fields: from text processing and CGI scripts to professional, large-scale programs.

As a programmer and a programming-language geek, I know what makes me happy while programming, and I designed Ruby with these elements in mind. I based the language on an object-oriented paradigm, provided a solid feature set (e.g., exceptions, iterators, etc.), and made sure to keep things consistent and balanced. Ruby will help you concentrate on solving problems. It is straightforward and not the least bit enigmatic.

It's my sincere hope that this book will help you enjoy programming in Ruby.

Happy programming!

—Yukihiro "Matz" Matsumoto
Japan

Table of Contents

Preface .... *ix*

Chapter 1—Introduction *1*

    Ruby's Elegance 1
    Ruby in Action 3

Chapter 2—Language Basics *5*

    Command-Line Options 5
    Environment Variables 7
    Lexical Conventions 8
    Literals 9
    Variables 15
    Operators 17
    Methods 20
    Control Structures 25
    Object-Oriented Programming 29
    Security 33

Chapter 3—Built-in Library Reference *36*

    Predefined Variables 36
    Predefined Global Constants 38
    Built-in Functions 39
    Built-in Library 47

Chapter 4—Standard Library Reference *110*

    Standard Library 110

Chapter 5—Ruby Tools *166*

    Standard Tools 166

    Additional Tools 173

    Ruby Application Archive 174

Chapter 6—Ruby Updates *176*

    Summary of Changes 176

    The Future of Ruby 178

    Participate in Ruby 179

Index *181*

Preface

Ruby in a Nutshell is a practical reference covering everything from Ruby syntax to the specifications of its standard class libraries. With portability and convenience in mind, I have arranged it into a concise tool that provides just the information you need while programming. Although this book is based on Ruby 1.6.5, its contents should remain applicable to future versions of Ruby, and many of the changes that will be included in Version 1.8 are shown in Chapter 6.

This book covers all the built-in features and standard bundled libraries of Ruby. It isn't an introductory book; rather it works best sitting top of your desk when you program in Ruby. The book assumes you have prior programming experience, preferably in Ruby. System programming experience may be required to understand some parts of the book, for example, network programming using sockets.

This book doesn't cover the Ruby C API for extending and embedding Ruby, nor does it cover additional libraries, e.g., those available from RAA (*http://www.ruby-lang.org/en/raa.html*). For information on these topics, please consult the online documents available at *http://www.ruby-lang.org*, other books, or you can wait for O'Reilly to publish books on them. :-)

How This Book Is Organized

Chapter 1, *Introduction*, briefly introduces the Ruby programming language, highlights the language features, and discusses what makes Ruby unique.

Chapter 2, *Language Basics*, describes Ruby language syntax and covers command-line options, environment variables, lexical convention, literals, variables, operators, methods, control structures, object-oriented programming, and security.

Chapter 3, *Built-in Library Reference*, describes the core functionality built into the standard Ruby interpreter. This part contains descriptions for more than 800 built-in methods in 42 classes and modules.

Chapter 4, *Standard Library Reference*, describes the useful libraries that come with the standard Ruby distribution, from network access via HTTP and CGI programming to data persistence using the DBM library.

Chapter 5, *Ruby Tools*, describes the tools that come with the standard Ruby distribution—debugger, profiler, and `irb` (Interactive Ruby)—and some useful tools not bundled with the Ruby standard distribution.

Chapter 6, *Ruby Updates*, describes the features added to the development version of Ruby (1.7). Those features aren't yet available in the current stable Version 1.6.5 but will be in the next stable version (1.8).

Conventions Used in This Book

The following conventions are used in this book:

Italic
> Used for strings to be replaced for particular value.

Constant width
> Indicates command-line options; environment variable names; fragments of Ruby code, i.e., names and reserved words, including method names, variable names, class names, etc.; examples; user input.

[ ] Text in brackets is usually optional.

... Text followed by an ellipsis can be any number of sequences of the text.

[...] or {...}
> Ellipses between brackets or braces refers to omitted text.

 The owl icon designates a note, which is an important aside to the nearby text.

 The turkey icon designates a warning relating to the nearby text.

Comments and Questions

Please address comments and questions concerning this book to the publisher:

> O'Reilly & Associates, Inc.
> 1005 Gravenstein Highway North
> Sebastopol, CA 95472
> (800) 998-9938 (in the United States or Canada)
> (707) 829-0515 (international/local)
> (707) 829-0104 (fax)

There is a web page for this book, which lists errata, examples, or any additional information. You can access this page at:

http://www.oreilly.com/catalog/ruby

To comment or ask technical questions about this book, send email to:

bookquestions@oreilly.com

For more information about books, conferences, Resource Centers, and the O'Reilly Network, see the O'Reilly web site at:

http://www.oreilly.com

Acknowledgments

I wish to thank the editors who made the impossible possible: Yumi Hayatsu for the original Japanese version and Laura Lewin for this English version. Without their efforts, you wouldn't be reading this book. The time I worked with Laura was fun and busy; she succeeded in driving the lazy programmer to do the work of a technical writer.

Thanks to David L. Reynolds, Jr., the translator of O'Reilly Japan's *Ruby Pocket Reference* (from which this book was derived). He not only decrypted the mysterious Oriental language but also fixed bugs in the book and polished up descriptions. I would also like to thank the technical reviewers, Colin Steele and Todd Faulkner; they helped take a pocket reference and expand it to the full-sized book you are reading.

Finally, thanks to my family, who endured their husband/father spending too many hours before the computer.

>   *—A wife of noble character who can find? She is worth far more than rubies.*
>
>   *Proverbs 31:10*

CHAPTER 1

Introduction

Ruby has been readily adopted by programmers in Japan and has had much documentation written for it in Japanese. As programmers outside of Japan learn about the benefits of Ruby, there is a growing need for documentation in English. The first book I wrote for O'Reilly, *Ruby Pocket Reference*, was in Japanese. Since then Ruby has changed significantly. To meet the needs of non-Japanese programmers, we translated, updated, and expanded *Ruby Pocket Reference* into *Ruby in a Nutshell*.

Ruby is an object-oriented programming language that makes programming both enjoyable and fast. With the easy-to-use interpreter, familiar syntax, complete object-oriented functionality, and powerful class libraries, Ruby has become a language that can be applied to a broad range of fields from text processing and CGI scripts to professional, large-scale programs.

While Ruby is easy to learn, there are many details that you can't be expected to remember. This book presents those details in a clean and concise format. It is a reference to keep next to your desktop or laptop, designed to make Ruby even easier to use.

For those of you who are new to Ruby, there are several online tutorials available to get you started: Ruby's home page (*www.ruby-lang.org*) is a good starting point as it offers Ruby tutorials and the Ruby Language FAQ.

Ruby's Elegance

Ruby is a genuine object-oriented scripting language designed from the ground up to support the OOP model.

Most modern languages incorporate aspects of object-oriented programming. Because Ruby was designed from the beginning to support OOP, most programmers feel it is elegant, easy to use, and a pleasure to program. Everything in Ruby is an object; there's no exception.

While Ruby is object-oriented, you can also use Ruby to do procedural programming. But as you do, Ruby is secretly turning your nifty procedures into methods on a globally accessible object.

Throughout the development of the Ruby language, I've focused my energies on making programming faster and easier. To do so, I developed what I call the *principle of least surprise*. All features in Ruby, including object-oriented features, are designed to work as ordinary programmers (e.g., me) expect them to work. Here are some of those features:

Interpretive programming
No compilation is needed; you can edit and feed your program to the interpreter. The faster development cycle helps you enjoy the programming process.

Dynamic programming
Almost everything in Ruby is done at runtime. Types of variables and expressions are determined at runtime as are class and method definitions. You can even generate programs within programs and execute them.

Familiar syntax
If you've been programming in Java, Perl, Python, C/C++, or even Smalltalk, Ruby's syntax is easy to learn. The following simple factorial function illustrates how easily you can decipher its meaning:

```
def factorial(n)
  if n == 0
    return 1
  else
    return n * factorial(n-1)
  end
end
```

Iterators
The iterator feature for loop abstraction is built into the language, which means a block of code can be attached to a method call. The method can call back the block from within its execution. For example, **Array** has the **each** method to iterate over its contents. With this feature, you don't need to worry about the loop counter or boundary condition.

```
ary = [1,2,3,4,5]
ary.each do |i|
  puts 1*2
end  # prints 2,3,4,8,10 for each line
```

A block is used not only for loops. It can be used for various purposes including the **select** method of **Array**, which uses blocks to choose values that satisfy conditions from contents:

```
ary = [1,2,3,4,5]
ary = ary.select do |i|
  i %2 == 0
end  # returns array of even numbers.
```

Exceptions

Just as you'd expect in a modern OOP language, Ruby provides language-level support for exception handling. For example, an attempt to open a file that doesn't exist raises an exception, so that your program doesn't run, assuming an unmet precondition. This feature obviously enhances the reliability of your programs. Exceptions can be caught explicitly using the rescue clause of the begin statement:

```
begin
  f = open(path)
rescue
  puts "#{path} does not exist."
  exit 1
end
```

Class libraries

Ruby comes with a strong set of bundled class libraries that cover a variety of domains, from basic datatypes (strings, arrays, and hashes) to networking and thread programming. The following program retrieves the current time string from the local host via a network socket connection:

```
require "socket"
print TCPSocket.open("localhost","daytime").gets
```

In addition to bundled libraries, if you go to *http://www.ruby-lang.org/en/raa.html* shows a list of the many unbundled useful libraries along with applications and documentation. Since Ruby is rather young, the number of libraries available is smaller than that of Perl, for example, but new libraries are becoming available each day.

Portable

Ruby ports to many platforms, including Unix, DOS, Windows, OS/2, etc. Ruby programs run on many platforms without modification.

Garbage collection

Object-oriented programming tends to allocate many objects during execution. Ruby's garbage collector recycles unused object automatically.

Built-in security check

Ruby's taint model provides safety when handling untrusted data or programs.

Ruby in Action

Like Python or Perl, Ruby is a scripting language. Scripting languages offer some great advantages over other languages, such as C++ and Java. They allow programmers to show off a lot of programming concepts and principles in a relatively small amount of space. Ruby does this, while maintaining code readability.

```
# the "Hello World."
print "Hello World.\n"

# output file contents in reverse order
print File::readlines(path).reverse

# print lines that contains the word "Ruby".
```

```ruby
while line = gets()
  if /Ruby/ =~ line
    print line
  end
end


# class and methods
class Animal
  def legs
    puts 4
  end
end

class Dog<Animal
  def bark
    puts "bow!"
  end
end

fred = Dog::new
fred.legs                # prints 4
fred.bark                # prints bow!

# exception handling
begin
  printf "size of %s is %d\n", path, File::size(path)
rescue
  printf "error! probably %s does not exist\n", path
end

# rename all files to lowercase names
ARGV.each {|path| File::rename(path, path.downcase)}

# network access
require 'socket'
print TCPSocket::open("localhost", "daytime").read

# Ruby/Tk
require 'tk'
TkButton.new(nil, 'text'=>'hello', 'command'=>'exit').pack
Tk.mainloop
```

CHAPTER 2

Language Basics

Ruby does what you'd expect it to do. It is highly consistent, and allows you to get down to work without having to worry about the language itself getting in your way.

Command-Line Options

Like most scripting language interpreters, Ruby is generally run from the command line. The interpreter can be invoked with the following options, which control the environment and behavior of the interpreter itself:

    ruby [*options*] [--] [*programfile*] [*argument...*]

-a Used with -n or -p to split each line. Split output is stored in $F.

-c Checks syntax only, without executing program.

-C *dir*
    Changes directory before executing (equivalent to -X).

-d Enables debug mode (equivalent to -debug). Sets $DEBUG to true.

-e *prog*
    Specifies *prog* as the program from the command line. Specify multiple -e options for multiline programs.

-F *pat*
    Specifies *pat* as the default separator pattern ($;) used by split.

-h Displays an overview of command-line options (equivalent to -help).

-i [*ext*]
    Overwrites the file contents with program output. The original file is saved with the extension *ext*. If *ext* isn't specified, the original file is deleted.

-I *dir*
    Adds *dir* as the directory for loading libraries.

-K [*kcode*]

Specifies the multibyte character set code (e or E for EUC (extended Unix code); s or S for SJIS (Shift-JIS); u or U for UTF-8; and a, A, n, or N for ASCII).

-l Enables automatic line-end processing. Chops a newline from input lines and appends a newline to output lines.

-n Places code within an input loop (as in while gets; ... end).

-0[*octal*]

Sets default record separator ($/) as an octal. Defaults to \0 if *octal* not specified.

-p Places code within an input loop. Writes $_ for each iteration.

-r *lib*

Uses require to load *lib* as a library before executing.

-s Interprets any arguments between the program name and filename arguments fitting the pattern -*xxx* as a switch and defines the corresponding variable.

$*xxx*.-S

Searches for a program using the environment variable PATH.

-T [*level*]

Sets the level for tainting checks (1 if level not specified). Sets the $SAFE variable.

-v Displays version and enables **verbose** mode (equivalent to --verbose).

-w Enables verbose mode. If programfile not specified, reads from STDIN.

-x [*dir*]

Strips text before #!ruby line. Changes directory to *dir* before executing if *dir* is specified.

-X *dir*

Changes directory before executing (equivalent to -c).

-y Enables parser debug mode (equivalent to --yydebug).

--copyright

Displays copyright notice.

--debug

Enables debug mode (equivalent to -d).

--help

Displays an overview of command-line options (equivalent to -h).

--version

Displays version.

--verbose

Enables verbose mode (equivalent to -v). Sets $VERBOSE to true.

--yydebug

Enables parser debug mode (equivalent to -y).

Single character command-line options can be combined. The following two lines express the same meaning:

```
ruby -ne 'print if /Ruby/' /usr/share/dict/words
ruby -n -e 'print if /Ruby/' /usr/share/dict/words
```

Environment Variables

In addition to using arguments and options on the command line, the Ruby interpreter uses the following environment variables to control its behavior. The ENV object contains a list of current environment variables.

DLN_LIBRARY_PATH
> Search path for dynamically loaded modules.

HOME
> Directory moved to when no argument is passed to Dir::chdir. Also used by File::expand_path to expand "~".

LOGDIR
> Directory moved to when no arguments are passed to Dir::chdir and environment variable HOME isn't set.

PATH
> Search path for executing subprocesses and searching for Ruby programs with the -S option. Separate each path with a colon (semicolon in DOS and Windows).

RUBYLIB
> Search path for libraries. Separate each path with a colon (semicolon in DOS and Windows).

RUBYLIB_PREFIX
> Used to modify the RUBYLIB search path by replacing prefix of library *path1* with *path2* using the format *path1*;*path2* or *path1path2*. For example, if RUBYLIB is:

> /usr/local/lib/ruby/site_ruby

> and RUBYLIB_PREFIX is:

> /usr/local/lib/ruby;f:/ruby

> Ruby searches f:/ruby/site_ruby. Works only with DOS, Windows, and OS/2 versions.

RUBYOPT
> Command-line options passed to Ruby interpreter. Ignored in taint mode (where $SAFE is greater than 0).

RUBYPATH
> With -S option, search path for Ruby programs. Takes precedence over PATH. Ignored in taint mode (where $SAFE is greater than 0).

RUBYSHELL

Specifies shell for spawned processes. If not set, SHELL or COMSPEC are checked.

Lexical Conventions

Ruby programs are composed of elements already familiar to most programmers: lines, whitespace, comments, identifiers, reserved words, literals, etc. Particularly for those programmers coming from other scripting languages such as Perl, Python or tcl, you'll find Ruby's conventions familiar, or at least straightforward enough not to cause much trouble.

Whitespace

We'll leave the thorny questions like "How much whitespace makes code more readable and how much is distracting?" for another day. If you haven't already caught onto this theme, the Ruby interpreter will do pretty much what you expect with respect to whitespace in your code.

Whitespace characters such as spaces and tabs are generally ignored in Ruby code, except when they appear in strings. Sometimes, however, they are used to interpret ambiguous statements. Interpretations of this sort produce warnings when the -w option is enabled.

a + b

Interpreted as a+b (a is a local variable)

a +b

Interpreted as a(+b) (a, in this case, is a method call)

Line Endings

Ruby interprets semicolons and newline characters as the ending of a statement. However, if Ruby encounters operators, such as +, -, or backslash at the end of a line, they indicate the continuation of a statement.

Comments

Comments are lines of annotation within Ruby code that are ignored at runtime. Comments extend from # to the end of the line.

```
# This is a comment.
```

Ruby code can contain embedded documents too. Embedded documents extend from a line beginning with =begin to the next line beginning with =end. =begin and =end must come at the beginning of a line.

```
=begin
This is an embedded document.
=end
```

Identifiers

Identifiers are names of variables, constants, and methods. Ruby distinguishes between identifiers consisting of uppercase characters and those of lowercase characters. Identifier names may consist of alphanumeric characters and the underscore character (_). You can distinguish a variable's type by the initial character of its identifier.

Reserved Words

The following list shows the reserved words in Ruby:

BEGIN	do	next	then
END	else	nil	true
alias	elsif	not	undef
and	end	or	unless
begin	ensure	redo	until
break	false	rescue	when
case	for	retry	while
class	if	return	yield
def	in	self	__FILE__
defined?	module	super	__LINE__

These reserved words may not be used as constant or local variable names. They can, however, be used as method names if a receiver is specified.

Literals

I've often wondered why we programmers are so enamored with literals. I'm waiting for the day when a language comes along and introduces "figuratives." In the interim, the rules Ruby uses for literals are simple and intuitive, as you'll see the following sections.

Numbers

Strings and numbers are the bread and butter of literals. Ruby provides support for both integers and floating-point numbers, using classes Fixnum, Bignum, and Float.

Integers

Integers are instances of class Fixnum or Bignum:

```
123                        # decimal
1_234                      # decimal with underline
0377                       # octal
0xff                       # hexadecimal
0b1011                     # binary
?a                         # character code for 'a'
12345678901234567890       # Bignum:  an integer of infinite length
```

Floating-point numbers

Floating-point numbers are instances of class `Float`:

```
123.4          # floating point value
1.0e6          # scientific notation
4E20           # dot not required
4e+20          # sign before exponential
```

Strings

A string is an array of bytes (octets) and an instance of class `String`:

`"abc"`
> Double-quoted strings allow substitution and backslash notation.

`'abc'`
> Single-quoted strings don't allow substitution and allow backslash notation only for \\ and \'.

String concatenation

Adjacent strings are concatenated at the same time Ruby parses the program.

```
"foo" "bar"          # means "foobar"
```

Expression substitution

`#$var` and `#@var` are abbreviated forms of `#{$var}` and `#{@var}`. Embeds value of expression in `#{...}` into a string.

Backslash notation

In double-quoted strings, regular expression literals, and command output, backslash notation can be represent unprintable characters, as shown in Table 2-1.

Table 2-1: Backslash notations

Sequence	Character represented
\n	Newline (0x0a)
\r	Carriage return (0x0d)
\f	Formfeed (0x0c)
\b	Backspace (0x08)
\a	Bell (0x07)
\e	Escape (0x1b)
\s	Space (0x20)
\\nnn	Octal notation (n being 0–7)
\\xnn	Hexadecimal notation (n being 0–9, a–f, or A–F)
\cx, \C-x	Control-x
\M-x	Meta-x (c | 0x80)
\M-\C-x	Meta-Control-x
\x	Character x

`command`

Converts command output to a string. Allows substitution and backslash notation

General delimited strings

The delimiter ! in expressions like this: `%q!...!` can be an arbitrary character. If the delimiter is any of the following: ([{ <, the end delimiter becomes the corresponding closing delimiter, allowing for nested delimiter pairs.

`%!foo!`
`%Q!foo!`

Equivalent to double quoted string `"foo"`

`%q!foo!`

Equivalent to single quoted string `'foo'`

`%x!foo!`

Equivalent to `` `foo` `` command output

here documents

Builds strings from multiple lines. Contents span from next logical line to the line that starts with the delimiter.

```
<<FOO

FOO
```

Using quoted delimiters after <<, you can specify the quoting mechanism used for String literals. If a minus sign appears between << and the delimiter, you can indent the delimiter, as shown here:

```
puts <<FOO          # String in double quotes ("")
    hello world
    FOO

    puts <<"FOO"     # String in double quotes ("")
    hello world
    FOO

    puts <<'FOO'     # String in single quotes ('')
    hello world
    FOO

    puts <<`FOO`     # String in backquotes (``)
    hello world
    FOO

    puts <<-FOO      # Delimiter can be indented
        hello world
        FOO
```

Symbols

A symbol is an object corresponding to an identifier or variable:

```
:foo            # symbol for 'foo'
:$foo           # symbol for variable '$foo'
```

Arrays

An array is a container class that holds a collection of objects indexed by an integer. Any kind of object may be stored in an array, and any given array can store a heterogeneous mix of object types. Arrays grow as you add elements. Arrays can be created using **array.new** or via literals. An array expression is a series of values between brackets []:

[]   An empty array (with no elements)

[1, 2, 3]
   An array of three elements

[1, [2, 3]]
   A nested array

General delimited string array

You can construct arrays of strings using the shortcut notation, **%W**. Only whitespace characters and closing parentheses can be escaped in the following notation:

```
%w(foo bar baz)     # ["foo", "bar", "baz"]
```

Hashes

A hash is a collection of key-value pairs or a collection that is indexed by arbitrary types of objects.

A hash expression is a series of **key=>value** pairs between braces.

```
{key1 => val1, key2 => val2}
```

Regular Expressions

Regular expressions are a minilanguage used to describe patterns of strings. A regular expression literal is a pattern between slashes or between arbitrary delimiters followed by **%r**:

```
/pattern/
/pattern/im         # option can be specified
%r!/usr/local!      # general delimited regular expression
```

Regular expressions have their own power and mystery; for more on this topic, see O'Reilly's *Mastering Regular Expressions* by Jeffrey E.F. Friedl.

Regular-expression modifiers

Regular expression literals may include an optional modifier to control various aspects of matching. The modifier is specified after the second slash character, as shown previously and may be represented by one of these characters:

i   Case-insensitive

o   Substitutes only once

x   Ignores whitespace and allows comments in regular expressions

m   Matches multiple lines, recognizing newlines as normal characters

Regular-expression patterns

Except for control characters, (+ ? . * ^ $ ( ) [ ] { } | \), all characters match themselves. You can escape a control character by preceding it with a backslash.

Regular characters that express repetition (* + { }) can match very long strings, but when you follow such characters with control characters ?, you invoke a nongreedy match that finishes at the first successful match (i.e., +, *, etc.) followed by ? (i.e., +?, *?, etc.).

^   Matches beginning of line.

$ Matches end of line.

.   Matches any single character except newline. Using m option allows it to match newline as well.

[...]
   Matches any single character in brackets.

[^...]
   Matches any single character not in brackets.

*re**
   Matches 0 or more occurrences of preceding expression.

re+
   Matches 1 or more occurrences of preceding expression.

re?
   Matches 0 or 1 occurrence of preceding expression.

re{n}
   Matches exactly *n* number of occurrences of preceding expression.

re{n,}
   Matches *n* or more occurrences of preceding expression.

re{n,m}
   Matches at least *n* and at most *m* occurrences of preceding expression.

a|b
   Matches either *a* or *b*.

(*re*)
   Groups regular expressions and remembers matched text.

`(?imx)`

Temporarily toggles on i, m, or x options within a regular expression. If in parentheses, only that area is affected.

`(?-imx)`

Temporarily toggles off i, m, or x options within a regular expression. If in parentheses, only that area is affected.

`(?:re)`

Groups regular expressions without remembering matched text.

`(?imx:re)`

Temporarily toggles on i, m, or x options within parentheses.

`(?-imx:re)`

Temporarily toggles off i, m, or x options within parentheses.

`(?#...)`

Comment.

`(?=re)`

Specifies position using a pattern. Doesn't have a range.

`(?!re)`

Specifies position using pattern negation. Doesn't have a range.

`(?>re)`

Matches independent pattern without backtracking.

`\w`   Matches word characters.

`\W`   Matches nonword characters.

`\s`   Matches whitespace. Equivalent to [\t\n\r\f].

`\S`   Matches nonwhitespace.

`\d`   Matches digits. Equivalent to [0–9].

`\D`   Matches nondigits.

`\A`   Matches beginning of string.

`\Z`   Matches end of string. If a newline exists, it matches just before newline.

`\z`   Matches end of string.

`\G`   Matches point where last match finished.

`\b`   Matches word boundaries when outside brackets. Matches backspace (0x08) when inside brackets.

`\B`   Matches nonword boundaries.

`\n`, `\t`, *etc.*

Matches newlines, carriage returns, tabs, etc.

`\1...\9`

Matches *n*th grouped subexpression.

`\10...`

Matches *n*th grouped subexpression if it matched already. Otherwise refers to the octal representation of a character code.

Variables

There are five types of variables in Ruby: global, instance, class, locals and constants. As you might expect, global variables are accessible globally to the program, instance variables belong to an object, class variables to a class and constants are, well... constant. Ruby uses special characters to differentiate between the different kinds of variables. At a glance, you can tell what kind of variable is being used.

Global Variables

`$foo`

Global variables begin with $. Uninitialized global variables have the value `nil` (and produce warnings with the -w option). Some global variables have special behavior. See the section "Predefined Variables" in Chapter 3.

Instance Variables

`@foo`

Instance variables begin with @. Uninitialized instance variables have the value `nil` (and produce warnings with the -w option).

Class Variables

`@@foo`

Class variables begin with @@ and must be initialized before they can be used in method definitions. Referencing an uninitialized class variable produces an error. Class variables are shared among descendants of the class or module in which the class variables are defined. Overriding class variables produce warnings with the -w option.

Local Variables

`foo`

Local variables begin with a lowercase letter or _. The scope of a local variable ranges from class, module, def, or do to the corresponding end or from a block's opening brace to its close brace {}. The scope introduced by a block allows it to reference local variables outside the block, but scopes introduced by others don't. When an uninitialized local variable is referenced, it is interpreted as a call to a method that has no arguments.

Constants

```
Foo
```

Constants begin with an uppercase letter. Constants defined within a class or module can be accessed from within that class or module, and those defined outside a class or module can be accessed globally. Constants may not be defined within methods. Referencing an uninitialized constant produces an error. Making an assignment to a constant that is already initialized produces a warning, not an error. You may feel it contradicts the name "constant," but remember, this is listed under "variables."

Pseudo-Variables

In addition to the variables discussed, there are also a few *pseudo-variables*. Pseudo-variables have the appearance of local variables but behave like constants. Assignments may not be made to pseudo-variables.

```
self
```
> The receiver object of the current method

```
true
```
> Value representing `true`

```
false
```
> Value representing `false`

```
nil
```
> Value representing "undefined"; interpreted as `false` in conditionals

```
__FILE__
```
> The name of the current source file

```
__LINE__
```
> The current line number in the source file

Assignment

```
target = expr
```

The following elements may assign targets:

Global variables
> Assignment to global variables alters global status. It isn't recommended to use (or abuse) global variables. They make programs cryptic.

Local variables
> Assignment to uninitialized local variables also serves as variable declaration. The variables start to exist until the end of the current scope is reached. The lifetime of local variables is determined when Ruby parses the program.

Constants
> Assignment to constants may not appear within a method body. In Ruby, reassignment to constants isn't prohibited, but it does raise a warning.

Attributes take the following form:

```
expr.attr
```

Assignment to attributes calls the *attr=* method of the result of *expr*.

Elements

Elements take the following form:

```
expr[arg...]
```

Assignment to elements calls the []= method of the result of *expr*.

Parallel Assignment

```
target[, target...][, *target] = expr[, expr...][, *expr]
```

Targets on the left side receive assignment from their corresponding expressions on the right side. If the last left-side target is preceded by *, all remaining right-side values are assigned to the target as an array. If the last right-side expression is preceded by *, the array elements of expression are expanded in place before assignment.

If there is no corresponding expression, nil is assigned to the target. If there is no corresponding target, the value of right-side expression is just ignored.

Abbreviated Assignment

```
target op= expr
```

This is the abbreviated form of:

```
target = target op expr
```

The following operators can be used for abbreviated assignment:

```
+=   -=   *=   /=   %=   **=   <<=   >>=   &=   |=   ^=   &&=   ||=
```

Operators

Ruby supports a rich set of operators, as you'd expect from a modern language. However, in keeping with Ruby's object-oriented nature, most operators are in fact method calls. This flexibility allows you to change the semantics of these operators wherever it might make sense.

Operator Expressions

Most operators are actually method calls. For example, a + b is interpreted as a.+(b), where the + method in the object referred to by variable a is called with b as its argument.

For each operator (+ - * / % ** & | ^ << >> && ||), there is a corresponding form of abbreviated assignment operator (+= -= etc.)

Here are the operators shown in order of precedence (highest to lowest):

```
::
[]
**
+(unary) -(unary) ! ~
 * / %
+ -
<< >>
&
| ^
> >= < <=
<=> == === != =~ !~
&&
||
.. ...
?:
= (and abbreviated assignment operators such as +=, -=, etc.)
not
and or
```

Nonmethod operators

The following operators aren't methods and, therefore, can't be redefined:

```
...
!
not
&&
and
||
or
::
=
+=, -=, (and other abbreviated assignment operators)
? : (ternary operator)
```

Range operators

Range operators function differently depending on whether or not they appear in conditionals, if expressions, and while loops.

In conditionals, they return true from the point right operand is true until left operand is true:

expr1 .. *expr2*
    Evaluates *expr2* immediately after *expr1* turns true.

expr1 ... *expr2*
    Evaluates *expr2* on the iteration after *expr1* turns true.

In other contexts, they create a range object:

expr1 .. *expr2*
> Includes both expressions (*expr1* <= x <= *expr2*)

expr1 ... *expr2*
> Doesn't include the last expression (*expr1* <= x < *expr2*)

Logical operators

If the value of the entire expression can be determined with the value of the left operand alone, the right operand isn't evaluated.

&& and
> Returns `true` if both operands are `true`. If the left operand is `false`, returns the value of the left operand, otherwise returns the value of the right operand.

|| or
> Returns `true` if either operand is `true`. If the left operand is `true`, returns the value of the left operand, otherwise returns the value of the right operand.

The operators and and or have extremely low precedence.

Ternary operator

Ternary ?: is the conditional operator. It's another form of the if statement.

a ? *b* : *c*
> If *a* is `true`, evaluates *b*, otherwise evaluates *c*. It's best to insert spaces before and after the operators to avoid mistaking the first part for the method *a*? and the second part for the symbol :*c*.

defined? operator

defined? is a special operator that takes the form of a method call to determine whether or not the passed expression is defined. It returns a description string of the expression, or `nil` if the expression isn't defined.

defined? *variable*
> True if *variable* is initialized
> ```
> foo = 42
> defined? foo     # => "local-variable"
> defined? $_      # => "global-variable"
> defined? bar     # => nil (undefined)
> ```

defined? *method_call*
> True if a method is defined (also checks arguments)
> ```
> defined? puts       # => "method"
> defined? puts(bar)  # => nil (bar is not defined here)
> defined? unpack     # => nil (not defined here)
> ```

defined? super
> True if a method exists that can be called with super
> ```
> defined? super      # => "super" (if it can be called)
> defined? super      # => nil     (if it cannot be)
> ```

```
defined? yield
```
True if a code block has been passed

```
defined? yield   # => "yield" (if there is a block passed)
defined? yield   # => nil     (if there is no block)
```

Methods

Methods are the workhorses of Ruby; all of your carefully crafted algorithms live in methods on objects (and classes). In Ruby, "method" means both the named operation (e.g. "dump") and the code that a specific class provides to perform an operation.

Strictly speaking, Ruby has no functions, by which I mean code not associated with any object. (In C++, this is what you might call a "global-scope function".) All code in Ruby is a method of some object. But Ruby allows you the flexibility of having some methods appear and work just like functions in other languages, even though behind the scenes they're still just methods.

Normal Method Calls

*obj.method([expr...[, *expr[, &expr]]])*

*obj.method [expr...[, *expr[, &expr]]]*

*obj::method([expr...[, *expr[, &expr]]])*

*obj::method [expr...[, *expr[, &expr]]]*

Calls a method. May take as arguments any number of *expr* followed by **expr* and *&expr*. The last expression argument can be a hash declared directly without braces. **expr* expands the array value of that expression and passes it to the method. *&expr* passes the `Proc` object value of that expression to the method as a block. If it isn't ambiguous, arguments need not be enclosed in parentheses. Either . or :: may be used to separate the object from its method, but it is customary in Ruby code to use :: as the separator for class methods.

*method([expr...[, *expr[, &expr]]])*

*method [expr...[, *expr[, &expr]]]*

Calls a method of `self`. This is the only form by which private methods may be called.

Within modules, module methods and private instance methods with the same name and definition are referred to by the general term *module functions*. This kind of method group can be called in either of the following ways:

```
Math.sin(1.0)
```

or:

```
include Math
sin(1.0)
```

You can append ! or ? to the name of a Ruby method. Traditionally, ! is appended to a method that requires more caution than the variant of the same name without !. A question mark ? is appended to a method that determines the state of a Boolean value, true or false.

Attempting to call a method without specifying either its arguments or parentheses in a context in which a local variable of the same name exists results in the method call being interpreted as a reference to the local variable, not a call to the method.

Specifying Blocks with Method Calls

Methods may be called with blocks of code specified that will be called from within the method.

method_call {[|[variable[, variable...]]|] code}

method_call do [|[variable[, variable...]]|] code end

Calls a method with blocks specified. The code in the block is executed after a value is passed from the method to the block and assigned to the variable (the block's argument) enclosed between ||.

A block introduces its own scope for new local variables. The local variables that appear first in the block are local to that block. The scope introduced by a block can refer local variables of outer scope; on the other hand, the scope introduced by class, module and def statement can't refer outer local variables.

The form {...} has a higher precedence than do ... end. The following:

    identifier1 identifier2 {|varizable| code}

actually means:

    identifier1(identifier2 {|variable| code})

On the other hand:

    identifier1 identifier2 do |variable| code end

actually means:

    identifier1(identifier2) do |variable| code end

def Statement

```
def method([arg..., arg=default..., *arg, &arg])
code
[rescue [exception_class[, exception_class...]] [=> variable] [then]
code]...
[else
code]
[ensure
code]
end
```

Defines a method. Arguments may include the following:

arg

> Mandatory argument.

arg=default

> Optional argument. If argument isn't supplied by that which is calling the method, the *default* is assigned to *arg*. The *default* is evaluated at runtime.

*arg

> If there are remaining actual arguments after assigning mandatory and optional arguments, they are assigned to *arg* as an array. If there is no remainder, empty array is assigned to *arg*.

&arg

> If the method is invoked with a block, it is converted to a **Proc** object, then assigned to *arg*. Otherwise, **nil** is assigned.

Operators can also be specified as method names. For example:

```
def +(other)
   return self.value + other.value
end
```

You should specify +@ or -@ for a single plus or minus, respectively. As with a **begin** block, a method definition may end with **rescue**, **else**, and **ensure** clauses.

Singleton Methods

In Ruby, methods can be defined that are associated with specific objects only. Such methods are called singleton methods. Singleton methods are defined using def statements while specifying a receiver.

Defines a singleton method associated with a specific object specified by a receiver. The *receiver* may be a constant (literal) or an expression enclosed in parentheses.

def Statement for Singleton Methods

```
def receiver.method([arg..., arg=default..., *arg, &arg])

code

[rescue [exception_class[, exception_class...]] [=> variable] [then]

  code]...

[else

  code]

[ensure

  code]

end
```

 A period . after *receiver* can be replaced by two colons (::).
They work the same way, but :: is often used for class methods.

A restriction in the implementation of Ruby prevents the definition of singleton methods associated with instances of the **Fixnum** or **Symbol** class.

```
a = "foo"
def a.foo
  printf "%s(%d)\n", self, self.size
end
a.foo      # "foo" is available for a only
```

Method Operations

Not only can you define new methods to classes and modules, you can also make aliases to the methods and even remove them from the class.

alias Statement

```
alias new old
```

Creates an alias *new* for an existing method, operator or global variable, specified by *old*. This functionality is also available via **Module#alias_method**. When making an alias of a method, it refers the current definition of the method.

```
def foo
  puts "foo!"
  end
alias foo_orig foo
def foo
  puts "new foo!"
```

```
end
foo                 # => "new foo!"
foo_orig            # => "foo!"
```

undef Statement

undef *method*...

Makes method defined in the current class undefined, even if the method is defined in the superclass. This functionality is also available via Module#undef_ method.

```
class Foo
def foo
end
end
class Bar<Foo
# Bar inherits "foo"
undef foo
end
b = Bar.new
b.foo      # error!
```

Other Method-Related Statements

The following statements are to be used within method definitions. The yield statement executes a block that is passed to the method. The super statement executes the overridden method of the superclass.

yield Statement

yield([*expr*...])

yield [*expr*...]

Executes the block passed to the method. The expression passed to yield is assigned to the block's arguments. Parallel assignment is performed when multiple expressions are passed. The output of the block, in other words the result of the last expression in the block, is returned.

super Statement

super

super([*expr*...])

super *expr*...

super executes the method of the same name in the superclass. If neither arguments nor parentheses are specified, the method's arguments are passed directly to the superclass method. In other words, a call to super(), which passes no arguments to the superclass method, has a different meaning from a call to super, where neither arguments nor parentheses are specified.

Control Structures

Ruby offers control structures that are pretty common to modern languages, but it also has a few unique ones.

if Statement

```
if conditional [then]
  code
[elsif conditional [then]
  code]...
[else
  code]
end
```

Executes *code* if the *conditional* is true. True is interpreted as anything that isn't false or nil. If the *conditional* isn't true, *code* specified in the else clause is executed. An if expression's *conditional* is separated from *code* by the reserved word then, a newline, or a semicolon. The reserved word if can be used as a statement modifier.

```
code if conditional
```

Executes *code* if conditional is true.

unless Statement

```
unless conditional [then]
  code
[else
  code]
end
```

Executes code if *conditional* is false. If the *conditional* is true, *code* specified in the else clause is executed. Like if, unless can be used as a statement modifier.

```
code unless conditional
```

Executes *code* unless *conditional* is true.

case Statement

```
case expression
[when expression[, expression...] [then]
 code]...
[else
 code]
end
```

Compares the *expression* specified by case and that specified by when using the === operator and executes the *code* of the when clause that matches. The *expression* specified by the when clause is evaluated as the left operand. If no when clauses match, case executes the *code* of the else clause. A when statement's *expression* is separated from *code* by the reserved word then, a newline, or a semicolon.

while Statement

```
while conditional [do]
 code
end
```

Executes *code* while *conditional* is true. A while loop's *conditional* is separated from *code* by the reserved word do, a newline,\, or a semicolon. The reserved word while can be used as statement modifier.

```
code while conditional
```

Executes *code* while *conditional* is true.

```
begin

  code

end while conditional
```

If a while modifier follows a begin statement with no rescue or ensure clauses, *code* is executed once before *conditional* is evaluated.

until Statement

```
until. conditional [do]
 code
end
```

Executes *code* while *conditional* is false. An until statement's *conditional* is separated from code by the reserved word do, a newline, or a semicolon. Like while, until can be used as statement modifier.

```
code until conditional
```

Executes *code* while *conditional* is false.

```
begin
    code
end until conditional
```

If an until modifier follows a **begin** statement with no **rescue** or **ensure** clauses, *code* is executed once before *conditional* is evaluated.

for Statement

```
for variable[, variable...] in expression [do]
  code
end
```

Executes *code* once for each element in *expression*. Almost exactly equivalent to:

```
    expression.each do |variable[, variable...]| code end
```

except that a **for** loop doesn't create a new scope for local variables. A **for** loop's *expression* is separated from *code* by the reserved word **do**, a newline, or a semicolon.

break Statement

```
break
```

Terminates a **while**/**until** loop. Terminates a method with an associated block if called within the block (with the method returning **nil**).

next Statement

```
next
```

Jumps to the point immediately before the evaluation of a loop's conditional. Terminates execution of a block if called within a block (with **yield** or call returning **nil**).

redo Statement

```
redo
```

Jumps to the point immediately after the evaluation of the loop's conditional. Restarts **yield** or **call** if called within a block.

retry Statement

retry

Repeats a call to a method with an associated block when called from outside a rescue clause.

Jumps to the top of a begin/end block if called from within a rescue clause.

begin Statement

```
begin
  code
[rescue [exception_class[, exception_class...]] [=> variable] [then]
  code]...
[else
  code]
[ensure
  code]
end
```

The begin statement encloses *code* and performs exception handling when used together with the rescue and ensure clauses.

When a rescue clause is specified, exceptions belonging to the *exception_class* specified are caught, and the *code* is executed. The value of the whole begin enclosure is the value of its last line of *code*. If no *exception_class* is specified, the program is treated as if the StandardError class had been specified. If a *variable* is specified, the exception object is stored to it. The rescue *exception_class* is separated from the rest of the code by the reserved word then, a newline, or a semicolon. If no exceptions are raised, the else clause is executed if specified. If an ensure clause is specified, its *code* is always executed before the begin/end block exits, even if for some reason the block is exited before it can be completed.

rescue Statement

code rescue *expression*

Evaluates the *expression* if an exception (a subclass of StandardError) is raised during the execution of the *code*. This is exactly equivalent to:

```
begin
  code
rescue StandardError
  expression
end
```

raise method

```
raise exception_class, message
raise exception_object
raise message
raise
```

Raises an exception. Assumes `RuntimeError` if no *exception_class* is specified. Calling `raise` without arguments in a `rescue` clause re-raises the exception. Doing so outside a rescue clause raises a message-less `RuntimeError`.

BEGIN Statement

```
BEGIN {
  code
}
```

Declares *code* to be called before the program is run.

END Statement

```
END {
  code
}
```

Declares *code* to be called at the end of the program (when the interpreter quits).

Object-Oriented Programming

Phew, seems like a long time since I introduced Ruby as "the object-oriented scripting language," eh? But now you have everything you need to get the nitty-gritty details on how Ruby treats classes and objects. After you've mastered a few concepts and Ruby's syntax for dealing with objects, you may never want to go back to your old languages, so beware!

Classes and Instances

All Ruby data consists of objects that are instances of some class. Even a class itself is an object that is an instance of the `Class` class. As a general rule, new instances are created using the `new` method of a class, but there are some exceptions (such as the `Fixnum` class).

```
a = Array::new
s = String::new
o = Object::new
```

class Statement

```
class class_name [< superclass]

  code

end
```

Defines a class. A *class_name* must be a constant. The defined class is assigned to that constant. If a class of the same name already exists, the class and *superclass* must match, or the *superclass* must not be specified, in order for the features of the new class definition to be added to the existing class. `class` statements introduce a new scope for local variables.

Methods

Class methods are defined with the `def` statement. The `def` statement adds a method to the innermost class or module definition surrounding the `def` statement. A `def` statement outside a class or module definition (at the top level) adds a method to the `Object` class itself, thus defining a method that can be referenced anywhere in the program.

When a method is called, Ruby searches for it in a number of places in the following order:

1. Among the methods defined in that object (i.e., singleton methods).
2. Among the methods defined by that object's class.
3. Among the methods of the modules included by that class.
4. Among the methods of the superclass.
5. Among the methods of the modules included by that superclass.
6. Repeats Steps 4 and 5 until the top-level object is reached.

Singleton Classes

Attribute definitions for a specific object can be made using the class definition construction. Uses for this form of class definition include the definition and a collection of singleton methods.

```
class << object

  code

end
```

Creates a virtual class for a specific object, defining the properties (methods and constants) of the class using the class definition construction.

Modules

A module is similar to a class except that it has no superclass and can't be instantiated. The `Module` class is the superclass of the `Class` class.

---

module Statement

```
module module_name

   code

end
```

A module statement defines a module. *module_name* must be a constant. The defined module is assigned to that constant. If a module of the same name already exists, the features of the new module definition are added to the existing module. module statements introduce a new scope for local variables.

Mix-ins

Properties (methods and constants) defined by a module can be added to a class or another module with the include method. They can also be added to a specific object using the extend method. See Module#include in the section "Classes and Modules" in Chapter 3, and the Object#extend in the section "Objects" in Chapter 3.

Method Visibility

There are three types of method visibility:

Public
   Callable from anywhere

Protected
   Callable only from instances of the same class

Private
   Callable only in functional form (i.e., without the receiver specified)

Method visibility is defined using the public, private, and protected methods in classes and modules.

public([symbol...])
   Makes the method specified by symbol public. The method must have been previously defined. If no arguments are specified, the visibility of all subsequently defined methods in the class or module is made public.

protected([symbol...])
   Makes the method specified by symbol protected. The method must have been previously defined. If no arguments are specified, the visibility of all subsequently defined methods in the class or module is made protected.

private([symbol...])
   Makes the method specified by symbol private. The method must have been previously defined. If no arguments are specified, the visibility of all subsequently defined methods in the class or module is made private.

Object Initialization

Objects are created using the new method of each object's class. After a new object is created by the new method, the object's `initialize` method is called with the arguments of the new method passed to it. Blocks associated with the new method are also passed directly to `initialize`. For consistency, you should initialize objects by redefining the `initialize` method, rather than the new method. The visibility of methods named `initialize` is automatically made private.

Attributes

Attributes are methods that can be referenced and assigned to externally as if they were variables. For example, the **Process** module attribute **egid** can be manipulated in the following way:

```
Process.egid      # Reference
Process.egid=id   # Assignment
```

These are actually two methods, one that takes no argument and another with a name ending with = that takes one argument. Methods that form such attributes are referred to as *accessor* methods.

Hooks

Ruby notifies you when a certain event happens, as shown in Table 2-2.

Table 2-2: Events and their hook methods

Event	Hook method	Of
Defining an instance method	`method_added`	Class
Defining a singleton method	`singleton_method_added`	Object
Make subclass	`inherited`	Superclass

These methods are called *hooks*. Ruby calls hook methods when the specific event occurs (at runtime). The default behavior of these methods is to do nothing. You have to override the method if you want to do something on a certain event:

```
class Foo
  def Foo::inherited(sub)
    printf "you made subclass of Foo, named %s\n", sub.name
  end
end
class Bar<Foo  # prints "you made subclass of Foo, named Bar"
end
```

There are other types of hook methods used by the mix-in feature. They are called by `include` and `extend` to do the actual mixing-in, as shown in Table 2-3. You can use these as hooks, but you have to call **super** when you override them.

Table 2-3: Mix-In hook methods

Event	Hook method	Of	From
Mixing in a module	`append_features`	Mix-in module	`Module#include`
Extending a object	`extend_object`	Mix-in module	`Object#extend`

Ruby 1.7 and later provide more hooks. See Chapter 6 for more information on future versions.

Security

Ruby is portable and can easily use code distributed across a network. This property gives you tremendous power and flexibility but introduces a commensurate burden: how do you use this capability without possibly causing damage?

Part of the answer lies in Ruby's security system, which allows you to "lock down" the Ruby environment when executing code that may be suspect. Ruby calls such data and code *tainted*. This feature introduces mechanisms that allow you to decide how and when potentially "dangerous" data or code can be used inside your Ruby scripts.

Restricted Execution

Ruby can execute programs with *security checking* turned on. The global variable `$SAFE` determines the level of the security check. The default safe level is 0, unless specified explicitly by the command-line option `-T`, or the Ruby script is run `setuid` or `setgid`.

`$SAFE` can be altered by assignment, but it isn't possible to lower the value of it:

```
$SAFE=1        # upgrade the safe level
$SAFE=4        #  upgrade the safe level even higher
$SAFE=0        # SecurityError! you can't do it
```

`$SAFE` is thread local; in other words, the value of `$SAFE` in a thread may be changed without affecting the value in other threads. Using this feature, threads can be sandboxed for untrusted programs.

```
Thread::start {      # starting "sandbox" thread
   $SAFE = 4         # for this thread only
   ...               # untrusted code
}
```

Level 0

Level 0 is the default safe level. No checks are performed on tainted data.

Any externally supplied string from `IO`, environment variables, and `ARGV` is automatically flagged as tainted.

The environment variable `PATH` is an exception. Its value is checked, and tainted only if any directory in it is writable by everybody.

Level 1

In this level, potentially dangerous operations using tainted data are forbidden. This is a suitable level for programs that handle untrusted input, such as CGI.

- Environment variables RUBYLIB and RUBYOPT are ignored at startup.

- Current directory (.) isn't included in $LOAD_PATH.

- The command-line options -e, -i, -I, -r, -s, -S, and -X are prohibited.

- Process termination if the environment variable PATH is tainted.

- Invoking methods and class methods of Dir, IO, File, and FileTest for tainted arguments is prohibited.

- Invoking test, eval, require, load, and trap methods for tainted argument is prohibited.

Level 2

In this level, potentially dangerous operations on processes and files are forbidden, in addition to all restrictions in level 1. The following operations are prohibited:

```
Dir::chdir
Dir::chroot
Dir::mkdir
Dir::rmdir
File::chown
File::chmod
File::umask
File::truncate
File#lstat
File#chmod
File#chown
File#truncate
File#flock
IO#ioctl
IO#fctrl
```
Methods defined in the FileTest module
```
Process::fork
Process::setpgid
Process::setsid
Process::setpriority
Process::egid=
Process::kill
```
load from a world-writable directory
```
syscall
exit!
trap
```

Level 3

In this level, all newly created objects are considered tainted, in addition to all restrictions in Level 2.

* All objects are created tainted.

* Object#untaint is prohibited.

* Proc objects retain current safe level to restore when their call methods are invoked.

Level 4

In this level, modification of global data is forbidden, in addition to all restrictions in Level 3. eval is allowed again in this level, since all dangerous operations are blocked in this level.

```
def safe_eval(str)
Thread::start {          # start sandbox thread
  $SAFE = 4              # upgrade safe level
  eval(str)             # eval in the sandbox
}.value                  # retrieve result
end

eval('1 + 1')            # => 2
eval('system "rm -rf /"') # SecurityError
```

The following operations are prohibited:

* Object#taint

* autoload, load, and include

* Modifying Object class

* Modifying untainted objects

* Modifying untainted classes or modules

* Retrieving meta information (e.g., variable list)

* Manipulating instance variables

* Manipulating threads other than current

* Accessing thread local data

* Terminating process (by exit, abort)

* File input/output

* Modifying environment variables

* srand

CHAPTER 3

Built-in Library Reference

We will now explore the core functionality that is built into the standard Ruby interpreter. You will find descriptions of more than 800 built-in methods in 42 classes and modules. Topics covered include predefined variables, predefined global constants, and built-in functions.

Predefined Variables

Ruby's predefined (built-in) variables affect the behavior of the entire program, so their use in libraries isn't recommended. The values in most predefined variables can be accessed by alternative means.

$!   The last exception object raised. The exception object can also be accessed using => in **rescue** clause.

$@   The **stack backtrace** for the last exception raised. The **stack backtrace** information can retrieved by **Exception#backtrace** method of the last exception.

$/   The input record separator (newline by default). **gets**, **readline**, etc., take their input record separator as optional argument.

$\   The output record separator (**nil** by default).

$,   The output separator between the arguments to print and **Array#join** (**nil** by default). You can specify separator explicitly to **Array#join**.

$;   The default separator for **split** (**nil** by default). You can specify separator explicitly for **String#split**.

$.   The number of the last line read from the current input file. Equivalent to **ARGF.lineno**.

$<   Synonym for **ARGF**.

$>   Synonym for $**defout**.

$0   The name of the current Ruby program being executed.

$$ The process.pid of the current Ruby program being executed.

$?   The exit status of the last process terminated.

$:   Synonym for $LOAD_PATH.

$DEBUG
   True if the -d or --debug command-line option is specified.

$defout
   The destination output for print and printf ($stdout by default).

$F   The variable that receives the output from split when -a is specified. This variable is set if the -a command-line option is specified along with the -p or -n option.

$FILENAME
   The name of the file currently being read from ARGF. Equivalent to ARGF.filename.

$LOAD_PATH
   An array holding the directories to be searched when loading files with the load and require methods.

$SAFE
   The security level. See the section "Security" in Chapter 2.

   0   No checks are performed on externally supplied (tainted) data. (default)

   1   Potentially dangerous operations using tainted data are forbidden.

   2   Potentially dangerous operations on processes and files are forbidden.

   3   All newly created objects are considered tainted.

   4   Modification of global data is forbidden.

$stdin
   Standard input (STDIN by default).

$stdout
   Standard output (STDOUT by default).

$stderr
   Standard error (STDERR by default).

$VERBOSE
   True if the -v, -w, or --verbose command-line option is specified.

$-x
   The value of interpreter option -x (x=0, a, d, F, i, K, l, p, v).

The following are local variables:

$_   The last string read by gets or readline in the current scope.

$~   MatchData relating to the last match. Regex#match method returns the last match information.

The following variables hold values that change in accordance with the current value of $~ and can't receive assignment:

$n ($1, $2, $3...)
> The string matched in the *n*th group of the last pattern match. Equivalent to *m*[*n*], where *m* is a `MatchData` object.

$&
> The string matched in the last pattern match. Equivalent to *m*[0], where *m* is a `MatchData` object.

$`
> The string preceding the match in the last pattern match. Equivalent to *m*.`pre_match`, where *m* is a `MatchData` object.

$'
> The string following the match in the last pattern match. Equivalent to *m*.`post_match`, where *m* is a `MatchData` object.

$+
> The string corresponding to the last successfully matched group in the last pattern match.

Predefined Global Constants

`TRUE`, `FALSE`, and `NIL` are backward-compatible. It's preferable to use `true`, `false`, and `nil`.

TRUE
> Synonym for `true`.

FALSE
> Synonym for `false`.

NIL
> Synonym for `nil`.

ARGF
> An object providing access to virtual concatenation of files passed as command-line arguments or standard input if there are no command-line arguments. A synonym for $<.

ARGV
> An array containing the command-line arguments passed to the program. A synonym for $*.

DATA
> An input stream for reading the lines of code following the __END__ directive. Not defined if __END__ isn't present in code.

ENV
> A hash-like object containing the program's environment variables. `ENV` can be handled as a hash.

RUBY_PLATFORM
> A string indicating the platform of the Ruby interpreter, e.g., `i686-linux`.

RUBY_RELEASE_DATE
> A string indicating the release date of the Ruby interpreter, e.g., `2001-09-19`.

RUBY_VERSION
> A string indicating the version of the Ruby interpreter, e.g., `1.6.5`.

STDERR
> Standard error output stream. Default value of `$stderr`.

STDIN
> Standard input stream. Default value of $stdin.

STDOUT
> Standard output stream. Default value of $stdout.

TOPLEVEL_BINDING
> A Binding object at Ruby's top level.

Built-in Functions

Since the Kernel module is included by Object class, its methods are available everywhere in the Ruby program. They can be called without a receiver (functional form), therefore, they are often called *functions*.

abort
> Terminates program. If an exception is raised (i.e., $! isn't nil), its error message is displayed.

Array(*obj*)
> Returns *obj* after converting it to an array using to_ary or to_a.

at_exit {...}
> Registers a block for execution when the program exits. Similar to END statement (referenced in the section "Control Structures" in Chapter 2), but END statement registers the block only once.

autoload(*classname, file*)
> Registers a class *classname* to be loaded from file the first time it's used. *classname* may be a string or a symbol.
>
>   autoload :Foo, "foolib.rb".

binding
> Returns the current variable and method bindings. The Binding object that is returned may be passed to the eval method as its second argument.

block_given?
> Returns true if the method was called with a block.

callcc {|*c*|...}
> Passes a Continuation object *c* to the block and executes the block. callcc can be used for global exit or loop construct.
>
> ```
> def foo(c)
>   puts "in foo"        #
>   c.call               # jump out
>   puts "out foo"       # this line never be executed
> end
> callcc{|c| foo(c)}     # prints "in foo"
> ```

caller([*n*])
> Returns the current execution stack in an array of the strings in the form *file:line*. If *n* is specified, returns stack entries from *n*th level on down.

catch(*tag*) {...}
> Catches a nonlocal exit by a throw called during the execution of its block.

```
def throwing(n)
  throw(:exit, n+2)
end

catch(:exit) {
  puts "before throwing"
  throwing(5)
  puts "after throwing"    # this line never be executed
} # returns 7
```

chomp([rs=$/])

Returns the value of variable $_ with the ending newline removed, assigning the result back to $_. The value of the newline string can be specified with *rs*.

```
$_ = "foo\n"
chomp                      # $_ => "foo"
$_ = "foo"
chomp                      # no chomp
```

chomp!([rs=$/])

Removes newline from $_, modifying the string in place.

chop

Returns the value of $_ with its last character (one byte) removed, assigning the result back to $_.

```
$_ = "foo\n"
chop                       # $_ => "foo"
$_ = "foo"
chop                       # $_ => "fo"
```

chop!

Removes the last character from $_, modifying the string in place.

eval(str[, scope[, file, line]])

Executes *str* as Ruby code. The binding in which to perform the evaluation may be specified with *scope*. The filename and line number of the code to be compiled may be specified using *file* and *line*.

exec(cmd[, arg...])

Replaces the current process by running the command *cmd*. If multiple arguments are specified, the command is executed with no shell expansion.

```
exec "echo *"              # wild card expansion
exec "echo", "*"           # no wild card expansion
```

exit([result=0])

Exits program, with *result* as the status code returned.

exit!([result=0])

Kills the program bypassing exit handling such as **ensure**, etc.

fail(...)

See raise(...)

Float(*obj*)

Returns *obj* after converting it to a float. Numeric objects are converted directly; nil is converted to 0.0; strings are converted considering 0x, 0b radix prefix. The rest are converted using *obj*.to_f.

```
Float(1)               # => 1.0
Float(nil)             # => 0.0
Float("1.5")           # => 1.5
Float("0xaa")          # => 170.0
```

fork
fork {...}

Creates a child process. nil is returned in the child process and the child process' ID (integer) is returned in the parent process. If a block is specified, it's run in the child process.

```
# traditional fork
if cpid = fork
  # parent process
else
  # child process
  exit!            # child process termination
end

# fork using a block
fork {
  # child process
  # child terminates automatically when block finish
}
```

format(*fmt*[, *arg*...])

See sprintf.

gets([*rs*=$/])

Reads the filename specified in the command line or one line from standard input. The record separator string can be specified explicitly with *rs*.

```
# easiest cat(1) imitation
while gets
  print $_            # gets updates $_
end
```

global_variables

Returns an array of global variable names.

gsub(*x*, *y*)
gsub(*x*) {...}

Replaces all strings matching *x* in $_ with *y*. If a block is specified, matched strings are replaced with the result of the block. The modified result is assigned to $_. See String#gsub in the next section.

gsub!(*x*, *y*)
gsub!(*x*) {...}

Performs the same substitution as gsub, except the string is changed in place.

Built-ins

`Integer(obj)`

> Returns *obj* after converting it to an integer. `Numeric` objects are converted directly; `nil` is converted to 0; strings are converted considering 0x, 0b radix prefix. The rest are converted using `obj.to_i`.

`Integer(1.2)`	`# => 1`
`Integer(1.9)`	`# => 1`
`Integer(nil)`	`# => 0`
`Integer("55")`	`# => 55`
`Integer("0xaa")`	`# => 170`

`lambda {|x|...}`
`proc {|x|...}`
`lambda`
`proc`

> Converts a block into a `Proc` object. If no block is specified, the block associated with the calling method is converted.

`load(file[, private=false])`

> Loads a Ruby program from *file*. Unlike `require`, it doesn't load extension libraries. If *private* is `true`, the program is loaded into an anonymous module, thus protecting the namespace of the calling program.

`local_variables`

> Returns an array of local variable names.

`loop {...}`

> Repeats a block of code.

`open(path[, mode="r"])`
`open(path[, mode="r"]) {|f|...}`

> Opens a *file*. If a block is specified, the block is executed with the opened stream passed as an argument. The file is closed automatically when the block exits. If *path* begins with a pipe |, the following string is run as a command, and the stream associated with that process is returned.

`p(obj)`

> Displays *obj* using its inspect method (often used for debugging).

`print([arg...])`

> Prints arg to `$defout`. If no arguments are specified, the value of `$_` is printed.

`printf(fmt[, arg...])`

> Formats *arg* according to *fmt* using `sprintf` and prints the result to `$defout`. For formatting specifications, see `sprintf` for detail.

`proc {|x|...}`
`proc`

> See `lamda`.

`putc(c)`

> Prints one character to the default output (`$defout`).

```
puts([str])
```
Prints string to the default output ($defout). If the string doesn't end with a newline, a newline is appended to the string.

```
puts "foo"       # prints: foo\n
puts "bar\n"     # prints: bar\n
```

```
raise(...)
fail(...)
```
Raises an exception. Assumes RuntimeError if no exception class is specified. Calling raise without arguments in a rescue clause re-raises the exception. Doing so outside a rescue clause raises a message-less RuntimeError. fail is an obsolete name for raise. See the section "raise method" in Chapter 2.

```
rand([max=0])
```
Generates a pseudo-random number greater than or equal to 0 and less than max. If max is either not specified or is set to 0, a random number is returned as a floating-point number greater than or equal to 0 and less than 1. srand may be used to initialize pseudo-random stream.

```
rand(10)     # => 8 (initialized by arbitrary seed)
srand(42)    # initialize pseudo random stream
rand         # => 0.7445250001
rand         # => 0.3427014787
srand(42)    # re-initialize pseudo random stream
rand         # => 0.7445250001 (repeated random value)
rand         # => 0.3427014787 (repeated random value)
```

```
readline([rs=$/])
```
Equivalent to gets except it raises an EOFError exception on reading EOF.

```
readlines([rs=$/])
```
Returns an array of strings holding either the filenames specified as command-line arguments or the contents of standard input.

```
require(lib)
```
Loads the library (including extension libraries) lib when it's first called. require will not load the same library more than once. If no extension is specified in lib, require tries to add .rb, .so, etc., to it.

```
scan(re)
scan(re) {|x|...}
```
Equivalent to $_.scan. See String#scan in the next section.

```
select(reads[, writes=nil[, excepts=nil[, timeout=nil]]])
```
Checks for changes in the status of three types of IO objects—input, output, and exceptions—which are passed as arrays of IO objects. nil is passed for arguments that don't need checking. A three-element array containing arrays of the IO objects for which there were changes in status is returned. nil is returned on timeout.

```
set_trace_func(proc)
```
Sets a handler for tracing. proc may be a string or Proc object. set_trace_func is used by the debugger and profiler.

sleep([*sec*])

> Suspends program execution for *sec* seconds. If *sec* isn't specified, the program is suspended forever.

```
sleep 1
sleep 1.5    # wait for 1.5 sec.
```

split([*sep*[, *max*]])

> Equivalent to $_.split. See String#split in the next section.

sprintf(*fmt*[, *arg*...])
format(*fmt*[, *arg*...])

> Returns a string in which *arg* is formatted according to *fmt*. Formatting specifications are essentially the same as those for sprintf in the C programming language. Conversion specifiers (% followed by conversion field specifier) in *fmt* are replaced by formatted string of corresponding argument.

> The following conversion specifiers, are supported by Ruby's format:

b   Binary integer

c   Single character

d,i Decimal integer

e   Exponential notation (e.g., 2.44e6)

E   Exponential notation (e.g., 2.44E6)

f   Floating-point number (e.g., 2.44)

g   use %e if exponent is less than -4, %f otherwise

G   use %E if exponent is less than -4, %f otherwise

o   Octal integer

s   String, or any object converted using to_s

u   Unsigned decimal integer

x   Hexadecimal integer (e.g., 39ff)

X   Hexadecimal integer (e.g., 39FF)

> Optional flags, width, and precision can be specified between % and conversion field specifiers.

```
sprintf("%s\n", "abc")      # => "abc\n"     (simplest form)
sprintf("d=%d", 42)         # => "d=42"      (decimal output)
sprintf("%04x", 255)        # => "00ff"      (width 4, zero padded)
sprintf("%8s", "hello")     # => "   hell"   (space padded)
sprintf("%.2s", "hello")    # => "he"        (trimmed by precision)
```

srand([*seed*])

> Initializes an array of random numbers. If *seed* isn't specified, initialization is performed using the time and other system information for the seed. Also see rand.

String(obj)

Returns *obj* after converting it to a string using *obj*.to_s.

```
String(1)              # => "1"
String(Object)         # => "Object"
String("1.5")          # => "1.5"
```

syscall(*sys*[, *arg*...])

Calls an operating system call function specified by number *sys*. The numbers and meaning of *sys* is system-dependant.

system(*cmd*[, *arg*...])

Executes *cmd* as a call to the command line. If multiple arguments are specified, the command is run directly with no shell expansion. Returns true if the return status is 0 (success).

```
system "echo *"        # wild card expansion
system "echo", "*"     # no wild card expansion
```

sub(*x*, *y*)
sub(*x*) {...}

Replaces the first string matching *x* in $_ with *y*. If a block is specified, matched strings are replaced with the result of the block. The modified result is assigned to $_. See String#sub in "Built-in Library" in Chapter 3.

sub!(*x*, *y*)
sub!(*x*) {...}

Performs the same replacement as sub, except the string is changed in place.

test(*test*, *f1*[, *f2*])

Performs one of the following file tests specified by the character *test*. In order to improve readability, you should use File class methods (for example File::readable?) rather than this function. Here are the file tests with one argument:

?r Is *f1* readable by the effective uid of caller?

?w Is *f1* writable by the effective uid of caller?

?x Is *f1* executable by the effective uid of caller?

?o Is *f1* owned by the effective uid of caller?

?R Is *f1* readable by the real uid of caller?

?W Is *f1* writable by the real uid of caller?

?X Is *f1* executable by the real uid of caller?

?O Is *f1* owned by the real uid of caller?

?e Does *f1* exist?

?z Does *f1* have zero length?

?s File size of *f1*(nil if 0)

?f Is *f1* a regular file?

?d Is *f1* a directory?

?l Is *f1* a symbolic link?

?p   Is *f1* a named pipe (FIFO)?

?S   Is *f1* a socket?

?b   Is *f1* a block device?

?c   Is *f1* a character device?

?u   Does *f1* have the **setuid** bit set?

?g   Does *f1* have the **setgid** bit set?

?k   Does *f1* have the sticky bit set?

?M   Last modification time for *f1*.

?A   Last access time for *f1*.

?C   Last **inode** change time for *f1*.

File tests with two arguments are as follows:

?=   Are modification times of *f1* and *f2* equal?

?>   Is the modification time of *f1* more recent than *f2*?

?<   Is the modification time of *f1* older than *f2*?

?-   Is *f1* a hard link to *f2*?

throw(*tag*[, *value=nil*])

    Jumps to the **catch** function waiting with the symbol or string *tag*. *value* is the return value to be used by **catch**.

trace_var(*var*, *cmd*)
trace_var(*var*) {...}

    Sets tracing for a global variable. The variable name is specified as a symbol. *cmd* may be a string or **Proc** object.

```
trace_var(:$foo) {|v|
  printf "$foo changed to %s\n", v
}
$foo = 55                    # prints: $foo changed to 55
```

trap(*sig*, *cmd*)
trap(*sig*) {...}

    Sets a signal handler. *sig* may be a string (like SIGUSR1) or an integer. SIG may be omitted from signal name. Signal handler for **EXIT** signal or signal number 0 is invoked just before process termination.

    cmd may be a string or **Proc** object. If *cmd* is IGNORE or SIG_IGN, the signal will be ignored. If *cmd* is DEFAULT or SIG_DFL, the default signal handler defined by the operating system will be invoked.

```
trap("USR1") {
  puts "receives SIGUSR1"
}
# prints message if SIGUSR1 is delivered to the process.
```

untrace_var(*var*[, *cmd*])

    Removes tracing for a global variable. If *cmd* is specified, only that command is removed.

Built-in Library

Ruby's built-in library provides you with a rich set of classes that form the foundation for your Ruby programs. There are classes for manipulating text (String), operating system services and abstractions (IO, File, Process, etc.), numbers (Integer, Fixnum, etc.), and so on.

Using these basic building blocks, you can build powerful Ruby programs. But wait, in the next chapter, I lay out the Standard Library, which extends Ruby's flexibility.

Objects

Ruby couldn't lay claim to being an "object-oriented scripting language" without providing fundamental tools for OOP. This basic support is provided through the Object class.

Object
Superclass of all classes

Object is the parent class of all other classes. When a method is defined at the top level, it becomes a private method of this class, making it executable by all classes as if it were a function in other languages.

Included Modules

Kernel

Private Instance Methods

initialize
> Initializes an object. Any block and arguments associated with the new method are passed directly to initialize. It's assumed that this method will be redefined by subclasses for object initialization.

Kernel
Module containing built-in functions

Kernel is the module in which Ruby's built-in functions are defined as module functions. Since it's included in Object, Kernel is indirectly included in all classes.

Private Instance Methods

Function-like methods are private methods of Kernel. Although the following methods fall into the same category, they are more similar to standard private instance methods than function-like methods.

remove_instance_variable(*name*)
> Removes instance variable specified by *name*.

Instance Methods

o == other
> Determines if the values are equal.

---

o === other
>   Comparison operator used by **case** statement (compares equality or confirms class membership).

o =~ other
>   Checks for pattern matches. The definition in **Kernel** calls ===.

o.class
o.type
>   Returns the class of the object *o*.

o.clone
>   Creates a copy of the object *o* (in as far as possible, including singleton methods).

o.display([*out*=$defout])
>   Prints the object. The output is specified in the argument.

o.dup
>   Creates a copy of the object (copying the content).

o.eql?(*obj*)
>   Performs a hash comparison. In order for **eql?** to return **true**, the **hash** value of both objects must have equal hash values.

o.equal?(*obj*)
>   Returns **true** if the two objects are the same.

o.extend(*mod*)
>   Adds module features (instance methods, etc.) of *mod* to the object *o*.

o.freeze
>   Freezes the object *o*, preventing further modification.

o.frozen?
>   Returns **true** if the object is frozen.

o.hash
>   Creates a hash value for the object *o*. Used together with **eql?** when the object is used as the key of a hash.

o.id
o.__id__
>   Returns the unique identifier value (integer) of the object *o*.

o.inspect
>   Returns the human readable string representation of the object *o*.

o.instance_eval(*str*)
o.instance_eval {...}
>   Evaluates the string or block in the context of the object. Features of the object, such as its instance variables, can be accessed directly.

o.instance_of?(*c*)
>   Returns **true** if *o* is an instance of the class *c*.

o.instance_variables
>   Returns an array of the object's instance variable names.

`o.kind_of?(mod)`

`o.is_a?(mod)`

> Returns `true` if the object is an instance of *mod,* one of its descendants, or includes *mod.*

`o.method(name)`

> Returns a `Method` object corresponding to *name.* An exception is raised if the corresponding method doesn't exist.

```
plus = 1.method(:+)
plus.call(2)      # => 3  (1+2)
```

`o.methods`

`o.public_methods`

> Returns an array of the object's public method names.

`o.nil?`

> Returns `true` if *o* is `nil`.

`o.private_methods`

> Returns an array of the object's private method names.

`o.protected_methods`

> Returns an array of the object's protected method names.

`o.public_methods`

> See `o.methods.`

`o.respond_to?(name)`

> Returns `true` if method named *name* exists in the object *o.*

`o.send(name[, arg...])`

`o.__send__(name[, arg...])`

> Calls the method named *name* in the object.

`o.singleton_methods`

> Returns an array of the object's singleton method names.

`o.taint`

> Marks the object as tainted (unsafe).

`o.tainted?`

> Returns `true` if the object *o* is tainted.

`o.to_a`

> Returns an array representation of the object *o.* For objects that can't be naturally converted into an array, an array containing that *o* as the sole element is returned.

`o.to_s`

> Returns a string representation of the object.

`o.type`

> See `o.class.`

`o.untaint`

> Removes the taint from the object.

Strings and Regular Expressions

Death, taxes, and ... processing text. Yes, these are virtually inescapable in a programmer's life. In Ruby, I share your pain. Using the `String`, `Regexp`, and `MatchData` classes, Ruby provides sharp tools to slice, dice, and manipulate text to your heart's content.

String Character String class

`String` is one of Ruby's basic datatypes, which contain arbitrary sequences of bytes. `String` can contain `\0`.

Included Module

`Enumerable, Comparable`

Class Method

`String::new(str)`
> Creates a string.

Instance Methods

Methods of the `String` class ending in `!` modify their receiver and return a string if modification took place, otherwise `nil`. Methods without a `!` return a modified copy of the string.

`~ s` Attempts to match pattern *s* against the `$_` variable. This method is obsolete.

`s % arg`
> An abbreviated form of `sprintf(s, arg...)`. Multiple elements are specified using an array.

`s * n`
> Returns a string consisting of *s* copied end to end *n* times.

`s + str`
> Returns a string with *str* concatenated to *s*.

`s << str`
> Concatenates *str* to *s*.

`s =~ x`
> Performs a regular expression match. If *x* is a string, it's turned into a `Regexp` object.

`s[n]`
> Returns the code of the character at position *n*. If *n* is negative, it's counted as an offset from the end of the string.

`s[n..m]`
`s[n, len]`
> Returns a partial string.
> ```
> "bar"[1..2]   # => "ar"
> "bar"[1..-1]  # => "ar"
> "bar"[-2..2]  # => "ar"
> "bar"[-2..-1] # => "ar"
> ```

```
"bar"[1,2]    # => "ar"
"bar"[-1, 1]  # => "r"
```

s[n]=value

Replaces the *n*th element in the string with *value*. *value* may be a character code or string.

s[n..m]=str
s[n, len]=str

Replaces a part of the string with *str*.

s.capitalize
s.capitalize!

Returns a copy of *s* with the first character converted to uppercase and the remainder to lowercase.

```
"fooBar".capitalize          # => "Foobar"
```

s.center(w)

Returns a string of length *w* with *s* centered in the middle. *s* is padded with spaces if it has a length of less than *w*.

```
"foo".center(10)             # => "   foo    "
"foo".center(2)              # => "foo"
```

s.chomp([rs=$/])
s.chomp!([rs=$/])

Deletes the record separator from the end of the string. The record separator string can be specified with *rs*.

```
"foo\n".chomp                # => "foo"
"foo".chomp                  # => "foo" (no chomp)
a = "foo\n"
a.chomp!                     # => "foo"
a                            # => "foo" (original changed)
a = "foo"
a.chomp!                     # => nil (no chomp)
```

s.chop
s.chop!

Deletes the last character (byte) from the string.

```
"foo\n".chop                 # => "foo"
"foo".chop                   # => "fo" (last byte chopped off)
```

s.concat(str)

Concatenates *str* to the string.

s.count(str...)

Returns the number of occurrences of the characters included in *str* (intersection of *str* if multiple *str* given) in *s*. *str* is negated if *str* starts with ^. The sequence c1-c2 means all characters between c1 and c2.

```
"123456789".count("2378")        # => 4
"123456789".count("2-8", "^4-6") # => 4
```

s.crypt(salt)

Encrypts the string *s* using a one way hash function. *salt* is a two-character string for seed. See **crypt(3)**.

```
s.delete(str...)
s.delete!(str...)
```
> Deletes the characters included in *str* (intersection of *str* if multiple *str* given) from *s*. Uses the same rules for building the set of characters as *s*.count.

```
"123456789".delete("2378")        # =>"14569"
"123456789".delete("2-8", "^4-6")  # =>"14569"
```

```
s.downcase
s.downcase!
```
> Replaces all uppercase characters in the string with lowercase characters.

```
s.dump
```
> Returns version of string with all nonprinting and special characters converted to backslash notation.

```
s.each([rs=$/]) {|line|...}
s.each_line([rs=$/]) {|line|...}
```
> Invokes the block for each line in *s*. The record separator string can be specified with *rs*.

```
s.each_byte {|byte|...}
```
> Invokes the block for each byte in *s*.

```
s.empty?
```
> Returns true if *s* has a length of 0.

```
s.gsub(x,y)
s.gsub(x) {...}
s.gsub!(x,y)
s.gsub!(x) {...}
```
> Replaces all strings matching *x* in the string with *y*. If a block is specified, matched strings are replaced with the result of the block.

```
"hello world".gsub(/[aeiou]/, ".")        # => "h.ll. w.rld"
"hello world".gsub(/[aeiou]/){|x|x.upcase} # => "hEllO wOrld"
```

```
s.hex
```
> Treats *s* as a string of hexadecimal digits and returns its integer value.

```
s.include?(x[, pos=0])
```
> Returns true if *str* is present in *s*. *x* may be an integer representing the character code, a string, or a regular expression. If *pos* is given, the search is started at offset *pos*.

```
s.index(x[, pos=0])
```
> Returns the index of *x* in string *s*, or nil if *x* isn't present. *x* may be an integer representing the character code, a string, or a pattern. If *pos* is given, the search is started at offset *pos*.

```
s.intern
```
> Returns the symbol corresponding to *s*.

```
s.length
```
> See *s*.size.

s.ljust(*w*)

    Returns a string of length *w* with *s* left-justified. *s* is padded with spaces if it has a length of less than *w*.

s.next
s.next!
s.succ
s.succ!

    Retrieves the next logical successor of the string *s*.

```
"aa".succ          # => "ab"
"99".succ          # => "100"
"a9".succ          # => "b0"
"Az".succ          # => "Ba"
"zz".succ          # => "aaa"
```

s.oct

    Treats *s* as a string of octal digits and returns its integer value. If *s* begins with 0x, it's treated as a hexidecimal string; if *s* begins with 0b, it's treated as a binary string.

s.replace(*str*)

    Replaces contents of *s* with that of *str*.

```
s = "abc"
s.replace("foobar")   # => "foobar"
s                     # => "foobar" (contents replaced)
```

s.reverse
s.reverse!

    Reverses the characters in the string *s*.

s.rindex(*x*[, *pos*])

    Returns the index of last occurrence of *x* in *s* as calculated from the end of the string, or nil if *x* isn't present. *x* may be an integer representing the character code, a string, or a pattern. If *pos* is given, the search is ended at offset *pos*.

s.rjust(*w*)

    Returns a string of length *w* with *s* right-justified. *s* is padded with spaces if it has a length of less than *w*.

```
"foo".rjust(10)    # => "       foo"
"foo".rjust(2)     # => "foo"
```

s.scan(*re*)
s.scan(*re*) {|*x*|...}

    Attempts to match the regular expression *re*, iterating through the string *s*. scan returns an array containing either arrays, which hold the matched results from groups, or strings, which represent the matched results if there were no groups in the expression. If a block is specified, it executes, iterating through each element in the array that would have been returned had *scan* been called without a block.

```
"foobarbaz".scan(/(ba)(.)/)  # => [["ba", "r"], ["ba", "z"]]
"foobarbaz".scan(/(ba)(.)/) {|s| p s}
```

```
# prints:
#   ["ba", "r"]
#   ["ba", "z"]
```

s.size
s.length
> Returns the length of the string.

s.slice(*n*)
s.slice(*n*..*m*)
s.slice(*n*, *len*)
> Returns a partial string.

s.slice!(*n*)
s.slice!(*n*..*m*)
s.slice!(*n*, *len*)
> Deletes the partial string specified and returns it.

```
a = "0123456789"
p a.slice!(1,2)     # "12"
p a                 # "03456789"
```

s.split([*sep*[, *max*]])
> Splits the contents of the string using *sep* as the delimiter and returns the
> resulting substrings as an array. If *sep* isn't specified, whitespace (or the value
> of $; if it isn't nil) is used as the delimiter. If *max* is specified, the string is
> split into a maximum of *max* elements.

```
"a b c".split           # => ["a","b","c"]
"a:b:c".split(/:/)      # => ["a","b","c"]
"a:b:c:::".split(/:/,4) # => ["a","b","c","",":"]
"a:b:c::".split(/:/,-1) # => ["a","b","c","",""]
"abc".split(//)         # => ["a","b","c"]
```

s.squeeze([*str*...])
s.squeeze!([*str*...])
> Reduces all running sequences of the same character included in *str* (inter-
> section of *str* if multiple *str* given) to a single character. If *str* isn't
> specified, running sequences of all characters are reduced to a single
> character.

```
"112233445".squeeze       # =>"12345"
"112233445".squeeze("1-3") # =>"123445"
```

s.strip
s.strip!
> Deletes leading and trailing whitespace.

s.sub(*x*, *y*)
s.sub(*x*) {...}
s.sub!(*x*, *y*)
s.sub!(*x*) {...}
> Replaces the first string matching *x* with *y*. If a block is specified, matched
> strings are replaced with the result of the block.

s.succ
> See *s*.next.

---

s.succ!

   See s.next.

s.sum([n=16])

   Returns an n-bit checksum of the string s.

s.swapcase
s.swapcase!

   Converts uppercase characters to lowercase and vice-versa.

s.to_f

   Converts the string into a floating point number. Returns 0.0 for uninterpretive string. For more strict conversion, use Float().

```
"1.5".to_f            # => 1.5
"a".to_f              # => 0.0
Float("a")            # error!
```

s.to_i

   Converts the string into an integer. Returns 0 for uninterpretive string. For
   more strict conversion, use Integer().

```
"1".to_i              # => 1
"a".to_i              # => 0
Integer("a")          # error!
```

s.to_str

   Returns s itself. Every object that has to_str method is treated as if it's a
   string.

s.tr(str, r)
s.tr!(str, r)

   Replaces the characters in str with the corresponding characters in r.

s.tr_s
s.tr_s!

   After replacing characters as in tr, replaces running sequences of the same
   character in sections that were modified with a single character.

```
"foo".tr_s("o", "f")              # => "ff"
"foo".tr("o", "f").squeeze("f")   # => "f"
```

s.succ

   See s.next.

s.succ!

   See s.next.

s.unpack(template)

   Unpacks s into arrays, decoding the string by performing the opposite of
   Array#pack(template). template can consist of a combination of the
   following directives:

   a   ASCII string

   A   ASCII string (deletes trailing spaces and null characters)

   b   Bit string (ascending bit order)

   B   Bit string (descending bit order)

c	Char
C	Unsigned char
d	Double (native format)
e	Little endian float (native format)
E	Little endian double (native format)
f	Float (native format)
g	Big endian float (native format)
G	Big endian double (native format)
h	Hex string (low nibble first)
H	Hex string (high nibble first)
i	Integer
I	Unsigned integer
l	Long
L	Unsigned long
m	Base64 encoded string
M	Quoted printable string
n	Big-endian short (network byte order)
N	Big-endian long (network byte order)
p	Pointer to a null-terminated string
P	Pointer to a structure (fixed-length string)
s	Short
S	Unsigned short
u	UU-encoded string
U	UTF-8 string
v	Little-endian short (VAX byte order)
V	Little-endian long (VAX byte order)
w	BER-compressed integer
x	Null byte
X	Backs up one byte
Z	ASCII string (deletes trailing null characters.)
@	Moves to absolute position

Each directive may be followed by a decimal number, indicating the number of elements to convert, or an asterisk, indicating that all remaining elements should be converted. Directives may be separated with a space. Directives sSiIlL followed by _ use the native size for that type on the current platform.

```
"\001\002\003\004".unpack("CCCC")    # => [1, 2, 3, 4]
"\001\002\003\004".unpack("V")       # => [67305985]
"\001\002\003\004".unpack("N")       # => [16909060]
```

s.upcase
s.upcase!

Replaces all lowercase characters in the string with uppercase characters.

s.upto(*max*) {|*x*| ...}

Returns *x* and continues to iterate to the next logical successor up to *max*. The method *s*.next is used to generate each successor.

```
"a".upto("ba") {|x|
  print x
}# prints a, b, c, ... z,aa, ... az, ba
```

Regexp

Regular expression class

Regex is object representation of regular expression. Regular expression is a mini-language to describe patterns of strings. For its syntax, see the section "Regular-expression patterns," which is under "Regular Expressions" in the "Literals" section in Chapter 2.

Class Methods

Regexp::new(*str*[, *option*[, *code*]])
Regexp::compile(*str*[, *option*[, *code*]])

Creates a Regexp object. *option* may be a logical OR of Regexp::IGNORECASE, Regexp::EXTENDED, and Regexp::MULTILINE. *code* may be a string specifying a multibyte character set code.

Regexp::escape(*str*)
Regexp::quote(*str*)

Returns a copy of *str* with all regular expression meta characters escaped.

Instance Methods

~ *r* Performs a regular expression match against $_. Equivalent to *r* =~ $_. This method is obsolete.

r === *str*

Synonym for *r* =~ *str* used in case statements.

r =~ *str*

Performs a regular expression match, returning the offset of the start of the match, or nil if the match failed.

r.casefold?

Returns true if the Regexp object is case-insensitive.

r.match(*str*)

Performs a regular expression match, returning the resulting match information as a MatchData object, or nil if the match failed.

```
if m = /fo*b.r+/.match(str)
    puts m[0]           # print matched string
end
```

r.source

Returns the original regular expression pattern string.

MatchData   Class for holding regular expression pattern match data

MatchData objects can be retrieved from the variable $~ or as return values from
Regexp.match.

Example

```
if m = pat.match(str)    # MatchData object on success
    print "matched: ", m[0], "\n"
    print "pre: ", m.pre_match, "\n"
    print "post: ", m.post_match, "\n"
end
```

Instance Methods

m[*n*]

Returns the match corresponding to the *n*th group of the regular expression.
If *n* is 0, the entire matched string is returned.

m.begin(*n*)

Returns the offset of the start of the match corresponding to the *n*th group of
the regular expression. If *n* is 0, the offset of the start of the entire matched
string is returned.

m.end(*n*)

Returns the offset of the end of the match corresponding to the *n*th group of
the regular expression. If *n* is 0, the offset of the end of the entire matched
string is returned.

m.length

See *m*.size

m.offset(*n*)

Returns a two-element array containing the beginning and ending offsets of
the string corresponding to the nth group of the regular expression.

m.post_match

Returns the part of the original string following the matched string.

m.pre_match

Returns the part of the original string preceding the matched string.

m.size
m.length

Returns the number of groups in the regular expression +1.

m.string
> Returns the original string used for the match.

m.to_a
> Returns an array of the matches (i.e., [$&, $1, $2...]).

Arrays and Hashes

One of the cornerstones of scripting languages is simple, flexible and powerful mechanisms for manipulating program data. In Ruby, the Array and Hash classes provide intuitive and rich capabilities for doing just that.

Array
Array class

Array is a class for an ordered collection of objects, indexed by integer. Any kind of object may be stored in an Array. Arrays grow as you add elements.

Included Module

Enumerable

Class Methods

Array[*x*...]
> Creates an array.

Array::new([*size*=0[, *fill*=nil]])
> Creates an array. Its *size* and initial values may also be specified.

>> Array::new(4, "foo")   # => ["foo","foo","foo","foo"]

Instance Methods

Methods of the Array class ending in ! modify their receiver and return an array if modification took place, otherwise nil. Methods without a ! return a modified copy of the array.

arr & *array*
> Returns an array of elements common to both arrays.

>> [1,3,5]|[1,2,3]   # => [1,3]

arr | *array*
> Returns an array combining elements from both arrays.

>> [1,3,5]|[2,4,6]   # => [1,2,3,4,5,6]

arr * *n*
> If *n* is an integer, returns a copy of array with *n* copies of *arr* concatenated to it. If *n* is a string, the equivalent of *arr*.join(*n*) is performed.

>> [5] * 3   # => [5, 5, 5].
>> ["foo", "bar"] * "-"   # => "foo-bar"

arr + *array*
> Returns a copy of *arr* with *array* concatenated to its end.

arr - *array*
> Returns a new array that is a copy of *arr*, removing any items in *array*.

>> [1, 2, 3, 4] - [2, 3]   # => [1, 4]

```
arr << item
```
Appends *item* to *arr*.

```
arr[n]
```
References the nth element of *arr*. If *n* is negative, it's interpreted as an offset from the end of *arr*.

```
arr[n..m]
arr[n,len]
```
Returns a partial string.

```
arr[n]=item
arr[r..m]=array
arr[r,len]=array
```
Assigns item or *arr* to the specified elements.

```
        arr = [0, 1, 2, 3, 4, 5]
        arr[0..2] = ["a", "b"]     # arr => ["a", "b", 3, 4, 5]
        arr[1, 0] = ["c"]          # arr => ["a", "c", "b", 3, 4, 5]
```

```
arr.assoc(key)
```
Searches through an array of arrays, returning the first array with an initial element matching *key*.

```
        a = [[1,2],[2,4],[3,6]]
        a.assoc(2)                 # => [2, 4]
```

```
arr.at(n)
```
Returns the nth element of *arr*.

```
arr.clear
```
Removes all elements from *arr*.

```
arr.collect {|x|...}
arr.collect! {|x|...}
arr.map {|x|...}
arr.map! {|x|...}
```
Invokes the block on each element returning an array holding the results.

```
        [1,2,3].collect{|x|x*2}    # => [2,4,6].
```

```
arr.compact
arr.compact!
```
Removes all nil elements from *arr*.

```
arr.concat(array)
```
Appends the elements of array to *arr*.

```
arr.delete(item)
arr.delete(item) {|item|...}
```
Deletes all elements matching *item* using ==. With a block, it returns the result of the block if no elements were deleted.

```
arr.delete_at(n)
```
Deletes the nth element of *arr*.

```
arr.delete_if {|x|...}
```
Deletes elements where the value of block is true.

```
arr.each {|x|...}
```
Invokes the block on each element of *arr*.

```
arr.each_index {|i|...}
```
Invokes the block on each element, passing the index, which is an integer ranging from 0 to `arr.length - 1`.

```
arr.empty?
```
Returns `true` if the array length is 0.

```
arr.fill(value[, beg[, len]]])
arr.fill(value, n..m)
```
Sets the specified element (or range of elements) in `arr` to `value`.

```
arr.first
```
Returns the first element of `arr`. Equivalent to `arr[0]`.

```
arr.flatten
arr.flatten!
```
Returns a flattened, one-dimensional array by moving all elements and subelements of `arr` into the new array.

```
[1, [2, 3, [4], 5]].flatten   #=> [1, 2, 3, 4, 5]
```

```
arr.include?(item)
arr.member?(item)
```
Returns `true` if `arr` contains item as an element.

```
arr.index(item)
```
Returns the index number of the first item in `arr` equal to item (with 0 being the first index number), or `nil` if item isn't present.

```
arr.indexes([index...])
arr.indices([index...])
```
Returns an array of elements from the specified indexes.

```
arr.join([s=$,])
```
Returns a string by joining together all elements in `arr`, separating each substring with `s`.

```
["foo", "bar"].join          # => "foobar"
["hello", "world"].join(" ") # => "hello world"
```

```
arr.last
```
Returns the last element of `arr`. Equivalent to `arr[-1]`.

```
arr.length
```
See `arr.size`

```
arr.map {|x|...}
```
See `arr.collect {|x|...}`

```
arr.map! {|x|...}
```
See `arr.collect {|x|...}`

```
arr.member?(item)
```
See `arr.include?(item)`

```
arr.nitems
```
Returns the number of elements with non-`nil` values.

`arr.pack(`*`template`*`)`

Packs the elements of an array into a string according to the directives in *template*. *template* may consist of a combination of these directives:

a   ASCII string (null padded)

A   ASCII string (space padded)

b   Bit string (ascending bit order)

B   Bit string (descending bit order)

c   Char

C   Unsigned char

d   Double (native format)

e   Little endian float (native format)

E   Little endian double (native format)

f   Float (native format)

g   Big endian float (native format)

G   Big endian double (native format)

h   Hex string (low nibble first)

H   Hex string (high nibble first)

i   Integer

I   Unsigned integer

l   Long

L   Unsigned long

m   Base64-encoded string

M   Quoted printable string

n   Big-endian short (network byte order)

N   Big-endian long (network byte order)

p   Pointer to a null-terminated string

P   Pointer to a structure (fixed-length string)

s   Short

S   Unsigned short

u   UU-encoded string

U   UTF-8 string

v   Little-endian short (VAX byte order)

V   Little-endian long (VAX byte order)

w   BER-compressed integer

x   Null byte

X   Backs up one byte

Z   ASCII string (space padded)

@   Moves to absolute position

Each directive may be followed by either a decimal number, indicating the number of elements to convert, or an asterisk, indicating that all remaining elements should be converted. Directives may be separated with a space. Directives sSiIlL followed by _ use the native size for that type on the current platform.

```
[1, 2, 3, 4].pack("CCCC")    # => "\001\002\003\004"
[1234].pack("V")             # => "\322\004\000\000"
[1234].pack("N")             # => "\000\000\004\322"
```

arr.pop

Removes the last element from *arr* and returns it.

arr.push(*obj*...)

Appends *obj* to *arr*.

arr.rassoc(*value*)

Searches through an array of arrays, returning the first array with a second element matching *value*.

```
[[1,2],[2,4],[3,6]].rassoc(2) # => [1, 2]
```

arr.reject {|*x*|...}

arr.reject! {|*x*|...}

Deletes elements where the value of block is true.

arr.replace(*array*)

Replaces the contents of *arr* with that of array.

arr.reverse

arr.reverse!

Puts the elements of the array in reverse order.

arr.reverse_each {|*x*|...}

Invokes the block on each element of *arr* in reverse order.

arr.rindex(*item*)

Returns the index of the last object in *arr* equal to item.

```
a = [1, 2, 3, 1, 3, 4]
a.rindex(3)                  #-> 4
a.rindex(9)                  #=> nil
```

arr.shift

Removes the first element from *arr* and returns it.

```
a = [1, 2, 3, 1, 3, 4]
a.shift                      #=> 1
a                            #=> [2, 3, 1, 3, 4]
```

arr.size

arr.length

Returns the number of elements in *arr*.

```
arr.slice(n)
arr.slice(n..m)
arr.slice(n, len)
```
Deletes the partial string specified and returns it.

```
a = "0123456789"
a.slice!(1,2)    # => "12"
a                # => "03456789"
```
```
arr.slice!(n)
arr.slice!(n..m)
arr.slice!(n, len)
```
Deletes the partial string specified and returns it.

```
a = [0,1,2,3,4]
a.slice!(4)      # => 4
a                # => [0,1,2,3]
a.slice!(1..2)   # => [1,2]
a                # => [0,3]
```
```
arr.sort
arr.sort!
```
Sorts the array.

```
arr.sort {|a, b| ...}
arr.sort! {|a, b| ...}
```
Arrays can be sorted by specifying the conditions for the comparison using a block. The block must compare *a* and *b*, returning 0 when *a* == *b*, a negative number when *a* < *b*, and a positive number when *a* > *b*.

```
arr.uniq
arr.uniq!
```
Deletes duplicate elements from **arr**.

```
arr.unshift(item)
```
Prepends *item* to *arr*.

```
a = [1,2,3]
a.unshift(0)        #=> [0,1,2,3]
```

Hash

Hash is a class for collection of key-value pairs, or in other words, a collection indexed by arbitrary type of objects, which define proper **hash** and **eql?** methods.

Included Module

Enumerable

Class Methods

```
Hash[key, value...]
```
Creates a Hash.

```
Hash[1,2,2,4]   # => {1=>2, 2=>4}
```

`Hash::new([default-nil])`

> Creates a Hash. A default value may also be specified.

```
h = Hash::new(15)    # => {}
h[44]                # => 15 (no key; default returned)
```

Instance Methods

Methods of the Hash class ending in a pipe ! modify their receiver and return a hash if modification took place, otherwise `nil`. Methods without a ! return a modified copy of the hash.

`h[key]`

> Returns the *value* associated with *key*.

`h[key]=value`

> Associates *value* with *key*.

`h.clear`

> Deletes all key-value pairs from *h*.

```
h = {1=>2, 2=>4}
h.clear
h                    # => {}
```

`h.default`

> Returns the default value for a key that doesn't exist. Note that the default value isn't copied, so that modifying the default object may affect all default values thereafter.

`h.default=value`

> Sets the default value.

`h.delete(key)`

> Deletes a key-value pair with a key equal to *key*.

`h.delete_if {|key, value| ...}`

> Deletes key-value pairs where the evaluated result of block is `true`.

```
h = {1=>2, 2=>4}
h.delete_if{|k,v| k % 2 == 0}
h              # => {1=>2}
```

`h.each {|key, value| ...}`
`h.each_pair {|key, value| ...}`

> Executes the block once for each key-value pair. Pairs are in unspecified order.

`h.each_key {|key| ...}`

> Executes the block once for each key. Keys are in unspecified order.

`h.each_value {|value| ...}`

> Executes the block once for each value. Values are in unspecified order.

`h.empty?`

> Returns `true` if the hash is empty.

`h.fetch(key[, ifnone=nil])`
`h.fetch(key) {|key| ...}`

> Returns the value associated with *key*. If *key* isn't present in *h*, the value of the block is returned. If no block is specified, *ifnone* is returned.

h.has_value?(*value*)
>   See *h*.value?(*value*)

h.index(*value*)
>   Returns the key for *value*, or nil if it isn't present.

```
h = {1=>2, 2=>4}
h.index(4)        # => 2
h.index(6)        # => nil
```

h.indexes([*key*...])
h.indices([*key*...])
>   Returns an array of values associated with the specified keys.

h.invert
>   Returns a hash containing *h*'s values as keys and *h*'s keys as values. If more than one keys have same value, arbitrary key is chosen.

```
h = {"y" => 365, "m" => 31, "d" => 24, "h" => 60}
p h.invert   # => {60=>"h", 365=>"y", 31=>"m", 24=>"d"}
```

h.key?(*key*)
h.has_key?(*key*)
h.include?(*key*)
h.member?(*key*)
>   Returns true if key is present in *h*.

h.keys
>   Returns an array of all keys.

h.rehash
>   Rebuilds the hash. If a hash isn't rebuilt after one of its key hash values is changed, that key will no longer be accessible.

```
a = [1,2]         # array as key
h = {a=>3}
h[a]              # => 3
a[0] = 2          # modify key
h[a]              # => nil (cannot find)
h.rehash
h[a]              # => 3
```

h.reject {|*key, value*|...}
h.reject! {|*key, value*|...}
>   Deletes key-value pairs where the value of block is true.

h.replace(*hash*)
>   Replaces the contents of *h* with that of *hash*.

h.shift
>   Removes a key-value pair from *h* and returns it.

h.size
h.length
>   Returns the number of key-value pairs in *h*.

h.sort
h.sort {|*a, b*|...}
>   Produces an array using *h*.to_a and returns it sorted.

```
h.store(key, value)
```
Synonym for h[key]=value.

```
h.to_a
```
Returns an array containing the array equivalent (key, value) of h.

```
h = {"y" => 365, "m" => 31, "d" => 24}
h.to_a        # => [["m", 31], ["d", 24], ["y", 365]]
```

```
h.to_hash
```
Returns h itself. Every object that has a to_hash method is treated as if it's a hash by h.replace and h.update.

```
h.update(hash)
```
Updates h with the contents of the specified hash. If duplicate keys exist, the associated value of hash takes precedence and overwrites that of h.

```
h1 = { "a" => 100, "b" => 200 }
h2 = { "b" => 300, "c" => 400 }
h1.update(h2)    #=> {"a"=>100, "b"=>300, "c"=>300}
```

```
h.value?(value)
h.has_value?(value)
```
Returns true if value is present in h.

```
h.values
```
Returns an array of all values.

```
h = {"y" => 365, "m" => 31, "d" => 24}
p h.values        # => [31, 24, 365]
```

Enumerable

The Enumerable module assumes that the including class has an each method. You can add the following methods to a class that provides each, by just including this module.

Instance Methods

```
e.collect {|x|...}
e.map {|x|...}
```
Returns an array containing the results of running the block on each item in e.

```
e.detect {|x|...}
```
See e.find {|x|...}

```
e.each_with_index {|x, i|...}
```
Executes the block once for each item in e, passing both the item and its index to the block.

```
["foo","bar","baz"].each_with_index {|x,i|
  printf "%d: %s\n", i, x
}
# prints:
#  0: foo
#  1: bar
#  2: baz.
```

```
e.entries
c.to_a
```
Returns an array containing the items passed to it by `e.each`.

```
e.find {|x|...}
e.detect {|x|...}
```
Returns the first item for which the block returns `true`.

```
["foo","bar","baz"].detect {|s| /^b/ =~ s} # => "bar"
```

```
e.find_all {|x|...}
e.select {|x|...}
```
Returns an array of all items for which the block returns `true`.

```
["foo","bar","baz"].select {|s| /^b/ =~ s} # => ["bar","baz"]
```

```
e.grep(re)
e.grep(re) {|x|...}
```
Returns an array containing all items matching `re`. Uses `===`. If a block is specified, it's run on each matching item, with the results returned as an array.

```
["foo","bar","baz"].grep(/^b/)   # => ["bar","baz"]
[1,"bar",4.5].grep(Numeric)      # => [1,4.5]
[1,"bar",4.5].grep(Numeric) {|x|
    puts x+1
}
# prints:
#  2
#  5.5
```

```
e.include?(item)
e.member?(item)
```
Returns `true` if an item equal to `item` is present in `e`. Items are compared using `==`.

```
e.map {|x|...}
```
See `e.collect {|x|...}`

```
e.max
```
Returns the item in `e` with the maximum value. Assumes a `<=>` comparison is possible between the items.

```
[1,5,3,2].max        # => 5
```

```
e.member?(item)
```
See `e.include?(item)`

```
e.min
```
Returns the item in `e` with the minimum value. Assumes a `<=>` comparison is possible between the items.

```
[1,5,3,2].min        # => 1
```

```
e.reject {|x|...}
```
Returns an array of all items for which the block returns `false`.

```
["foo","bar","baz"].reject {|s| /^b/ =~ s} # => ["foo"]
```

```
e.select {|x|...}
```
See `e.find_all {|x|...}`

```
e.sort
e.sort {|a, b| ...}
```
Returns an array of sorted items from e. If a block is specified, it's used for the comparison. Like <=>, the block must compare the two items and return a positive number (a> b), 0(a == b), or a negative number (a<b).

```
e.to_a
```
See e.entries

Numbers

As you'd expect, Ruby provides a suitably powerful set of classes for manipulating numeric data, through the classes Numeric, Integer, Fixnum, Bignum, and Float. In addition, further tools are available in the Precision and Math modules for manipulating numeric data.

Numeric   Superclass of all concrete numbers

Numeric provides common behavior of numbers. Numeric is an abstract class, so you should not instansiate this class.

Included Module

Comparable

Instance Methods

+n   Returns n.

-n   Returns n negated.

```
n + num
n - num
n * num
n / num
```
Performs arithmetic operations: addition, subtraction, multiplication, and division.

```
n % num
```
Returns the modulus of n.

```
n ** num
```
Exponentiation.

```
n.abs
```
Returns the absolute value of n.

```
n.ceil
```
Returns the smallest integer greater than or equal to n.

```
n.coerce(num)
```
Returns an array containing num and n both possibly converted to a type that allows them to be operated on mutually. Used in automatic type conversion in numeric operators.

n.divmod(*num*)

Returns an array containing the quotient and modulus from dividing *n* by *num*.

n.floor

Returns the largest integer less than or equal to *n*.

```
1.2.floor          #=> 1
2.1.floor          #=> 2
(-1.2).floor       #=> -2
(-2.1).floor       #=> -3
```

n.integer?

Returns true if *n* is an integer.

n.modulo(*num*)

Returns the modulus obtained by dividing *n* by *num* and rounding the quotient with floor. Equivalent to *n*.divmod(*num*)[1].

n.nonzero?

Returns *n* if it isn't zero, otherwise nil.

n.remainder(*num*)

Returns the remainder obtained by dividing *n* by *num* and removing decimals from the quotient. The result and n always have same sign.

```
(13.modulo(4))       #=>  1
(13.modulo(-4))      #=> -3
((-13).modulo(4))    #=>  3
((-13).modulo(-4))   #=> -1

(13.remainder(4))    #=>  1
(13.remainder(-4))   #=>  1
((-13).remainder(4)) #=> -1
(-13).remainder(-4)) #=> -1
```

n.round

Returns *n* rounded to the nearest integer.

```
1.2.round          #=> 1
2.5.round          #=> 3
(-1.2).round       #=> -1
(-2.5).round       #=> -3
```

n.truncate

Returns *n* as an integer with decimals removed.

```
1.2.truncate       #=> 1
2.1.truncate       #=> 2
(-1.2).truncate    #=> -1
(-2.1).truncate    #=> -2
```

n.zero?

Returns zero if *n* is 0.

Integer   Integer class

Integer provides common behavior of integers (Fixnum and Bignum). Integer is an abstract class, so you should not instansiate this class.

Inherited Class

Numeric

Included Module

Precision

Class Method

Integer::induced_from(numeric)
>   Returns the result of converting numeric into an integer.

Instance Methods

~ *i* Bitwise operations: AND, OR, XOR, and inversion.

i & *int*
i | *int*
i ^ *int*
i << *int*
i >> *int*
>   Bitwise left shift and right shift.

i[*n*]
>   Returns the value of the *n*th bit from the least significant bit, which is *i*[0].

```
5[0]      # => 1
5[1]      # => 0
5[2]      # => 1.
```

i.chr
>   Returns a string containing the character for the character code *i*.

```
65.chr    # => "A"
?a.chr    # => "a"
```

i.downto(*min*) {|*i*|...}
>   Invokes the block, decrementing each time from *i* to *min*.

```
3.downto(1) {|i|
  puts i
}
# prints:
#  3
#  2
#  1
```

i.next
i.succ
>   Returns the next integer following *i*. Equivalent to *i* + 1.

i.size
>   Returns the number of bytes in the machine representation of *i*.

i.step(*upto*, *step*) {|*i*|...}
>   Iterates the block from *i* to *upto*, incrementing by *step* each time.

```
10.step(5, -2) {|i|
  puts i
}
# prints:
```

```
# 10
# 8
# 6
```

i.succ

See *i*.next

i.times {|*i*| ...}

Iterates the block *i* times.

```
3.times {|i|
  puts i
}
# prints:
# 0
# 1
# 2  .
```

i.to_f

Converts *i* into a floating point number. Float conversion may lose precision information.

```
1234567891234567.to_f   # => 1.234567891e+15
```

i.to_int

Returns *i* itself. Every object that has **to_int** method is treated as if it's an integer.

i.upto(*max*) {|*i*| ...}

Invokes the block, incrementing each time from *i* to *max*.

```
1.upto(3) {|i|
  puts i
}
# prints:
# 1
# 2
# 3
```

Fixnum   Fixed-length number class

Fixnum objects are fixed-length numbers with a bit length of either 31 bits or 63 bits. If an operation exceeds this range, it's automatically converted to a **Bignum**.

Inherited Class

Integer

Bignum   Infinite-length integer class

Bignum objects are infinite-length integers capable of handling numbers as large as memory can hold. Conversions between **Fixnum** and **Bignum** integers are performed automatically.

Inherited Class

Integer

Float

Float objects represent floating-point numbers. They use double precision floating-point numbers as internel representation of the platform architecture.

Inherited Class

Numeric

Included Module

Precision

Class Method

Float::induced_from(*num*)
> Returns the result of converting *num* to a floating-point number.

Instance Methods

f.finite?
> Returns true if *f* isn't infinite and *f*.nan is false.

f.infinite?
> Returns 1 if *f* is positive infinity, -1 if negative infinity, or nil if anything else.

f.nan?
> Returns true if *f* isn't a valid IEEE floating point number.

Precision

Precision is a module to provide a conversion system between numbers.

Instance Methods

prec(*c*)
> Returns the result of converted self to the precision of class *c*. The definition in the Precision module actually returns *c*.induced_from(self).

prec_f
> Equivalent to prec(Float).

prec_i
> Equivalent to prec(Integer).

Comparable

The Comparable module assumes that the including class has a <=> method defined. The <=> method compares two objects and returns a positive number if the left operand is greater, 0 if it's equal to the right operand, or a negative number if it's smaller. You can add the following methods to a class that provides <=>, by just including this module.

Instance Methods

c < other

Returns true if c is less than *other* (i.e., *c <=> other* returns a negative number).

c <= other

Returns true if c is less than or equal to *other* (i.e., *c <=> other* returns either a negative number or 0).

c > other

Returns true if *c* is greater than *other* (i.e., *c <=> other* returns a positive number).

c >= other

Returns true if *c* is greater than or equal to *other* (i.e., *c <=> other* returns either a positive number or 0).

c == other

Returns true if the objects are equal (i.e., *c <=> other* returns 0).

c.between?(min, max)

Returns true if *c* is between *min* and *max.*

Math   Module of math functions

The Math module provides a collection of math functions. The Math module defines private instance methods and module methods that possess the same name and definition.

Module Functions

atan2(x, y)

Calculates the arc tangent.

cos(x)

Calculates the cosine of *x.*

exp(x)

Calculates an exponential function (e raised to the power of *x*).

frexp(x)

Returns a two-element array containing the nominalized fraction and exponent of *x.*

ldexp(x, exp)

Returns the value of *x* times 2 to the power of *exp.*

log(x)

Calculates the natural logarithm of *x.*

log10(x)

Calculates the base 10 logarithm of *x.*

sin(x)

Calculates the sine of *x.*

sqrt(*x*)
> Returns the square root of *x*. *x* must be positive.

tan(*x*)
> Calculates the tangent of *x*.

Constants

E   e, the base of natural logarithms

π   pi; the Ludolphian number

Operating System Services

Ruby's portability necessitates some level of abstraction between your Ruby scripts and the underlying operating system. Abstractions of I/O, filesystems and processes are provided through the Ruby built-in classes IO, File, File::Stat, FileTest, Dir, and Process.

IO   I/O class

IO is object-oriented representation of stdio. IO is a superclass of other IO related classes, such as File, BasicSocket, etc.

Included Module

Enumerable

Class Methods

IO::foreach(*path*) {|*x*|...}
> Opens the file and executes the block once for each line, closing the file when the block exits.
>
> ```
> n = 1
> IO::foreach(path) {|line|
>   print n, ":", lib
>   n+=1
> }
> ```

IO::new(*fd*[,*mode*="r"])
> Returns a new IO stream for the specified integer file descriptor *fd*.

IO::pipe
> Creates a pair of IO streams connected to each other and returns them as an array ([readIO, writeIO]).

IO::popen(*cmd*[,*mode*="r"])
IO::popen(*cmd*[,*mode*="r"]) {|*io*|...}
> Executes the command specified by *cmd* as a subprocess and creates an associated stream connected to it. If *cmd* is -, a new instance of Ruby is started as a subprocess with an IO object returned in the parent and nil returned in the child process. If a block is specified, it's run with the IO object as a parameter. The stream is closed when the block exits.

IO::readlines(*path*)
> Returns the contents of a file as an array of strings.

IO::select(*reads*[, *writes*=nil[, *excepts*=nil[,*timeout*=nil]]])

Checks for changes in the status of three types of IO objects, input, output, and exceptions, which are passed as arrays of IO objects. nil is passed for arguments that don't need checking. A three-element array containing arrays of the IO objects for which there were changes in status is returned. nil is returned on timeout.

```
IO::select([STDIN], nil, nil, 1.5)   # wair data for STDIN for 1.5 sec
```

Instance Methods

io << *str*

Prints *str* to *IO*.

io.binmode

Enables binary mode (for use on DOS/Windows). Once a stream is in binary mode, it can't be reset to non-binary mode.

io.close

Closes the *io*.

io.close_read

Closes the read-only end of a duplex IO stream.

io.close_write

Closes the write-only end of a duplex IO stream.

io.closed?

Returns true if *io* is closed.

io.each { |*x*| ... }
io.each_line { |*x*| ... }

Reads in the contents of *io* one line at a time, invoking the block each time.

```
f = open(path)
n = 1
f.each_line {|line|
  print n, ":", lib
  n+=1
}.
```

io.each_byte { |*x*| ... }

Reads in the contents of *io* one byte at a time, invoking the block each time.

io.eof
io.eof?

Returns true if EOF has been reached.

io.fcntl(*req*[, *arg*])

Calls fcntl(2) system call. Arguments and results are platform dependent. Not implemented on all platforms.

io.fileno
io.to_i

Returns the file descriptor number for *io*.

io.flush

Flushes output buffers.

io.getc

> Reads one character (8-bit byte) from *io* and returns its character code. Returns `nil` on EOF.

io.gets([*rs*=$/])

> Reads one line from *io*. Returns `nil` on EOF.

io.ioctl(*req*[, *arg*])

> Calls `ioctl(2)` system call. Arguments and results are platform dependent. Not implemented on all platforms.

io.isatty

> See *io*.tty?

io.lineno

> Returns the current line number in *io*.

io.lineno=n

> Sets the current line number in *io*.

io.pid

> Returns the process ID associated with *io*. Returns `nil` if no process exists.

io.pos
io.tell

> Returns the current position of the file pointer.

io.pos=*offset*

> Sets the position of the file pointer.

io.print(*arg*...)

> Writes the specified arguments to *io*.

io.printf(*fmt*[, *arg*...])

> Writes the specified arguments to *io* after formatting them. For formatting specifiers, see `sprintf` in "Built-in Functions" in Chapter 3.

io.putc(*c*)

> Writes one character to *io*.

io.puts(*str*)

> Writes *str* to *io*, appending `newline` if *str* doesn't end with `newline`.

```
io.puts("foo")      # prints "foo" and newline
io.puts("bar\n")    # prints "bar" and newline
```

io.read([*len*])

> Reads only the specified number of bytes from *io*. If *len* isn't specified, the entire file is read.

io.readchar

> Reads one character (8-bit byte) from *io*. Raises an exception on EOF.

io.readline([*rs*=$/])

> Reads one line from *io*. Raises an exception on EOF.

io.readlines([*rs*=$/])

> Reads all lines in *io* and returns them in an array.

io.reopen(*f*)

> Resets *io* to a copy of *f*. The class of *io* may be changed as well.

io.rewind
> Moves the file pointer to the beginning of *io*.

io.seek(*pos*[, *whence*=IO::SEEK_SET])
> Moves the file pointer. The starting point *whence* may be set to IO::SEEK_SET (beginning of stream), IO::SEEK_CUR (current position) or IO::SEEK_END (end of stream).

io.stat
> Calls fstat(2) system call and returns a File::Stat object.

io.sync
> Returns true if sync mode is enabled for output. In sync mode, the buffer is flushed after each write.

io.sync=*mode*
> Sets the sync mode for output to true or false.

io.sysread(*len*)
> Reads *len* bytes from *io* using read(2) system call. sysread should not be mixed with other reading IO methods.

io.syswrite(*str*)
> Writes *str* to *io* using write(2) system call. syswrite should not be mixed with other writing IO methods, or you may get unpredictable results.

io.tell
> See *io*.pos

io.to_i
> See *io*.fileno

io.to_io
> Returns *io* itself. Every object that has to_io method is treated as if it's an IO by IO::select and *io*.reopen.

io.tty?
io.isatty
> Returns true if *io* is connected to tty (terminal device).

io.ungetc(*c*)
> Pushes one character back onto *io*.

io.write(*str*)
> Writes *str* to *io*. Every object that has a write method can be assigned to $defout, the default output destination.

File
File class

A File represents an stdio object that connected to a regular file. open returns an instance of this class for regular files.

Inherited Class

IO

Class Methods

`File::atime(path)`
> Returns the last access time for *path*.

`File::basename(path[, suffix])`
> Returns the filename at the end of *path*. If *suffix* is specified, it's deleted from the end of the filename.

```
File.basename("/home/matz/bin/ruby.exe")          #=> "ruby.exe"
File.basename("/home/matz/bin/ruby.exe", ".exe") #=> "ruby"
```

`File::blockdev?(path)`
> Returns `true` if *path* is a block device.

`File::chardev?(path)`
> Returns `true` if *path* is a character device.

`File::chmod(mode, path...)`
> Changes the permission mode of the specified files.

`File::chown(owner, group, path...)`
> Changes the owner and group of the specified files.

`File::ctime(path)`
> Returns the last inode change time for *path*.

`File::delete(path...)`
`File::unlink(path...)`
> Deletes the specified files.

`File::directory?(path)`
> Returns `true` if *path* is a directory.

`File::dirname(path)`
> Returns the directory portion of *path*, without the final filename.

`File::executable?(path)`
> Returns `true` if *path* is executable.

`File::executable_real?(path)`
> Returns `true` if *path* is executable with real user permissions.

`File::exist?(path)`
> Returns `true` if *path* exists.

`File::expand_path(path[, dir])`
> Returns the absolute path of *path*, expanding ~ to the process owner's home directory, and *~user* to the *user*'s home directory. Relative paths are resolved from the directory specified by *dir*, or the current working directory if *dir* is omitted.

`File::file?(path)`
> Returns `true` if *path* is a regular file.

`File::ftype(`*path*`)`
> Returns one of the following strings representing a file type:

`file`
> Regular file

`directory`
> Directory

`characterSpecial`
> Character special file

`blockSpecial`
> Block special file

`fifo`
> Named pipe (FIFO)

`link`
> Symbolic link

`socket`
> Socket

`unknown`
> Unknown file type

`File::grpowned?(`*path*`)`
> Returns `true` if *path* is owned by the user's group.

`File::join(`*item...*`)`
> Returns a string consisting of the specified items joined together with `File::Separator` separating each item.

```
File::join("", "home", "matz", "bin") # => "/home/matz/bin"
```
`File::link(`*old, new*`)`
> Creates a hard link to file *old*.

`File::lstat(`*path*`)`
> Same as stat, except that it returns information on symbolic links themselves, not the files they point to.

`File::mtime(`*path*`)`
> Returns the last modification time for *path*.

`File::new(`*path*`[, `*mode*`="r"])`
`File::open(`*path*`[, `*mode*`="r"])`
`File::open(`*path*`[, `*mode*`="r"]) {|`*f*`|...}`
> Opens a file. If a block is specified, the block is executed with the new file passed as an argument. The file is closed automatically when the block exits. These methods differ from `Kernel#open` in that even if *path* begins with |, the following string isn't run as a command.

`File::owned?(`*path*`)`
> Returns `true` if *path* is owned by the effective user.

`File::pipe?(`*path*`)`
> Returns `true` if *path* is a pipe.

`File::readable?`(*path*)
> Returns `true` if *path* is readable.

`File::readable_real?`(*path*)
> Returns `true` if *path* is readable with real user permissions.

`File::readlink`(*path*)
> Returns the file pointed to by *path.*

`File::rename`(*old*, *new*)
> Changes the filename from *old* to *new.*

`File::setgid?`(*path*)
> Returns `true` if *path*'s set-group-id permission bit is set.

`File::setuid?`(*path*)
> Returns `true` if *path*'s set-user-id permission bit is set.

`File::size`(*path*)
> Returns the file size of *path.*

`File::size?`(*path*)
> Returns the file size of *path,* or `nil` if it's 0.

`File::socket?`(*path*)
> Returns `true` if *path* is a socket.

`File::split`(*path*)
> Returns an array containing the contents of *path* split into `File::dirname`(*path*) and `File::basename`(*path*).

`File::stat`(*path*)
> Returns a `File::Stat` object with information on *path.*

`File::sticky?`(*path*)
> Returns `true` if *path*'s sticky bit is set.

`File::symlink`(*old*, *new*)
> Creates a symbolic link to file *old.*

`File::symlink?`(*path*)
> Returns `true` if *path* is a symbolic link.

`File::truncate`(*path*, *len*)
> Truncates the specified file to *len* bytes.

`File::unlink`(*path...*)
> See `File::delete`(*path...*)

`File::umask`([*mask*])
> Returns the current umask for this process if no argument is specified. If an argument is specified, the umask is set, and the old umask is returned.

`File::utime`(*atime*, *mtime*, *path...*)
> Changes the access and modification times of the specified files.

`File::writable?`(*path*)
> Returns `true` if *path* is writable.

```
File::writable_real?(path)
```
Returns true if path is writable with real user permissions.

```
File::zero?(path)
```
Returns true if the file size of path is 0.

Instance Methods

```
f.atime
```
Returns the last access time for f.

```
f.chmode(mode)
```
Changes the permission mode of f.

```
f.chown(owner, group)
```
Changes the owner and group of f.

```
f.ctime
```
Returns the last inode change time for f.

```
f.flock(op)
```
Calls flock(2). op may be 0 or a logical or of the File class constants LOCK_
EX, LOCK_NB, LOCK_SH, and LOCK_UN.

```
f.lstat
```
Same as stat, except that it returns information on symbolic links themselves, not the files they point to.

```
f.mtime
```
Returns the last modification time for f.

```
f.path
```
Returns the pathname used to create f.

```
f.reopen(path[, mode="r"])
```
Reopens the file.

```
f.truncate(len)
```
Truncates f to len bytes.

Constants

Constants in the File class are also defined in the module File::Constants so
that they may be included separately if necessary.

open constants

> RDONLY
>> Read-only mode

> WRONLY
>> Write-only mode

> RDWR
>> Read and write mode

> APPEND
>> Append mode

CREAT
   Create file

EXCL
   Exclusive open

ioctl constants
NONBLOCK
   Nonblocking mode

TRUNC
   Truncate to 0 bytes

NOCTTY
   Don't allow a terminal device to become the controlling terminal

BINARY
   Binary mode

SYNC
   Sync mode

flock constants
LOCK_EX
   Exclusive lock

LOCK_NB
   Don't block when locking

LOCK_SH
   Shared lock

LOCK_UN
   Unlock

File::Stat   File status class

`File::Stat` contains file status information given by `File#stat` and other similar methods.

Included Module

`Comparable`

Instance Methods

s <=> stat
   Compares the modification times of *s* and *stat*.

s.atime
   Returns the last access time for *s*.

s.blksize
   Returns the block size of *s*'s file system.

s.blockdev?
   Returns `true` if *s* is a block device.

`s.blocks`
> Returns the number of blocks allocated to *s*.

`s.chardev?`
> Returns `true` if *s* is a character device.

`s.ctime`
> Returns the last `inode` change time for *s*.

`s.dev`
> Returns an integer representing the device on which *s* is located.

`s.directory?`
> Returns `true` if *s* is a directory.

`s.executable?`
> Returns `true` if *s* is executable.

`s.executable_real?`
> Returns `true` if *s* is executable with real user permissions.

`s.file?`
> Returns `true` if *s* is a regular file.

`s.ftype`
> Returns one of the following strings representing a file type of *s*:

> `file`
>> Regular file

> `directory`
>> Directory

> `characterSpecial`
>> Character special file

> `blockSpecial`
>> Block special file

> `fifo`
>> Named pipe (FIFO)

> `link`
>> Symbolic link

> `socket`
>> Socket

> `unknown`
>> Unknown file type

`s.gid`
> Returns the group ID.

`s.grpowned?`
> Returns `true` if *s* is owned by the user's group.

`s.ino`
> Returns the `inode` number for *s*.

`s.mode`
> Returns the access permission mode for *s*.

`s.mtime`
> Returns the modification time for `s`.

`s.nlink`
> Returns the number of hard links to `s`.

`s.owned?`
> Returns `true` if `s` is owned by the effective user.

`s.pipe?`
> Returns `true` if `s` is a pipe.

`s.rdev`
> Returns an integer representing the device type on which `s` is located.

`s.readable?`
> Returns `true` if `s` is readable.

`s.readable_real?`
> Returns `true` if `s` is readable with real user permissions.

`s.setgid?`
> Returns `true` if `s`'s set-group-id permission bit is set.

`s.setuid?`
> Returns `true` if `s`'s set-user-id permission bit is set.

`s.size`
> Returns the file size of `s`

`s.size?`
> Returns the file size of `s`, or `nil` if it's 0.

`s.socket?`
> Returns `true` if `s` is a socket.

`s.sticky?`
> Returns `true` if `s`'s sticky bit is set.

`s.symlink?`
> Returns `true` if `s` is a symbolic link.

`s.uid`
> Returns the user ID.

`s.writable?`
> Returns `true` if `s` is writable.

`s.writable_real?`
> Returns `true` if `s` is writable with real user permissions.

`s.zero?`
> Returns `true` if the file size of `s` is 0.

FileTest   File testing module

The `FileTest` module contains methods for testing files. The methods in this module are also provided as class methods of the `File` class.

Module Functions

blockdev?(*path*)
>   Returns true if *path* is a block device.

chardev?(*path*)
>   Returns true if *path* is a character device.

directory?(*path*)
>   Returns true if *path* is a directory.

executable?(*path*)
>   Returns true if *path* is executable.

executable_real?(*path*)
>   Returns true if *path* is executable with real user permissions.

exist?(*path*)
>   Returns true if *path* exists.

file?(*path*)
>   Returns true if *path* is a regular file.

grpowned?(*path*)
>   Returns true if *path* is owned by the user's group.

owned?(*path*)
>   Returns true if *path* is owned by the effective user.

pipe?(*path*)
>   Returns true if *path* is a pipe.

readable?(*path*)
>   Returns true if *path* is readable.

readable_real?(*path*)
>   Returns true if *path* is readable with real user permissions.

setgid?(*path*)
>   Returns true if *path*'s set-group-id permission bit is set.

setuid?(*path*)
>   Returns true if *path*'s set-user-id permission bit is set.

size(*path*)
>   Returns the file size of *path*.

size?(*path*)
>   Returns the file size of *path* or nil if it's 0.

socket?(*path*)
>   Returns true if *path* is a socket.

sticky?(*path*)
>   Returns true if *path*'s sticky bit is set.

symlink?(*path*)
>   Returns true if *path* is a symbolic link.

writable?(*path*)
>   Returns true if *path* is writable.

`writable_real?(path)`

Returns `true` if *path* is writable with real user permissions.

`zero?(path)`

Returns `true` if the file size of *path* is 0.

Dir

A `Dir` is a class to represent a directory stream that gives filenames in the directory in the operating system. `Dir` class also holds directory related operations, such as wild card filename matching, changing current working directory, etc. as class methods

Included Module

`Enumerable`

Class Methods

`Dir[pat]`
`Dir::glob(pat)`

Returns an array of filenames matching the specified wildcard pattern *pat*:

*   Matches any string including the null string

**   Matches any string recursively

?   Matches any single character

`[...]`

Matches any one of enclosed characters

`{a,b...}`

Matches any one of strings

```
Dir["foo.*"]      # matches "foo.c", "foo.rb", etc.
Dir["foo.?"]      # matches "foo.c", "foo.h", etc.
Dir["*.[ch]"]     # matches "main.c", "ruby.h", etc.
Dir["*.{rb,c}"]   # matches "main.c", "config.rb", etc.
Dir["**/*.c"]     # recursively matches any ".c" file
```

`Dir::chdir(path)`

Changes the current directory.

`Dir::chroot(path)`

Changes the root directory (only allowed by super user). Not available on all platforms.

`Dir::delete(path)`

See `Dir::rmdir(path)`.

`Dir::entries(path)`

Returns an array of filenames in directory path.

`Dir::foreach(path) {|f|...}`

Executes the block once for each file in the directory specified by path.

`Dir::getwd`
`Dir::pwd`
>Returns the current directory.

`Dir::glob(pat)`
>See `Dir[pat]`.

`Dir::mkdir(path[, mode=0777])`
>Creates the directory specified by *path*. Permission *mode* may be modified by the value of `File::umask` and is ignored on Win32 platforms.

`Dir::new(path)`
`Dir::open(path)`
`Dir::open(path) {|dir|...}`
>Returns a new directory object for *path*. If `open` is given a block, a new directory object is passed to the block, which closes the directory object before terminating.

`Dir::pwd`
>See `Dir::getwd`.

`Dir::rmdir(path)`
`Dir::unlink(path)`
`Dir::delete(path)`
>Deletes the directory specified by *path*. The directory must be empty.

Instance Methods

`d.close`
>Closes the directory stream.

`d.each {|f|...}`
>Executes the block once for each entry in *d*.

`d.pos`
`d.tell`
>Returns the current position in *d*.

`d.pos=offset`
>Sets the position in the directory stream.

`d.pos=pos`
`d.seek(pos)`
>Moves to a position in *d*. *pos* must be a value returned by `d.pos` or 0.

`d.read`
>Returns the next entry from *d*.

`d.rewind`
>Moves position in *d* to the first entry.

`d.seek(pos)`
>See `d.pos=pos`.

`d.tell`
>See `d.pos`.

Process

The `Process` module provides methods to manipulate processes. Some operations are platform dependent.

Module Methods

`Process.egid`
> Returns the effective group ID of this process.

`Process.egid=`*gid*
> Sets the effective group ID of this process.

`Process.euid`
> Returns the effective user ID of this process.

`Process.euid=`*uid*
> Sets the effective user ID of this process.

`Process.gid`
> Returns the group ID of this process.

`Process.gid=`*gid*
> Sets the group ID of this process.

`Process.pid`
> Returns the process ID of this process.

`Process.ppid`
> Returns the process ID of the parent of this process.

`Process.uid`
> Returns the user ID of this process.

`Process.uid=`*uid*
> Sets the user ID of this process.

Module Functions

`exit!([`*result*`=0])`
> Kills the program bypassing exit handling such as **ensure**, etc.

`fork`
`fork {...}`
> Creates a child process. `nil` is returned in the child process, and the child process' ID (`Integer`) is returned in the parent process. If a block is specified, it's executed in the child process.

`getpgid(`*pid*`)`
> Returns the process group ID for process *pid*. pid 0 means the current process ID.

`getpgrp([`*pid*`=$$])`
> Returns the process group ID for this process.

`getpriority(`*which, who*`)`
> Returns the current priority.

`kill(`*`sig, pid...`*`)`
> Sends signal to a process. *sig* is specified with a string such as KILL or an integer.

`setpgid(`*`pid`*`)`
> Sets the process group ID for process *pid*.

`setpgrp`
> Equivalent to `setpgid(0,0)`.

`setpriority(`*`which, who, prio`*`)`
> Sets process priority.

`setsid`
> Establishes this process as a new session.

`wait`
> Waits for a child process to exit and returns its process ID.

`wait2`
> Waits for a child process to exit and returns its process ID and exit status as an array.

`waitpid(`*`pid`*`[, `*`flags`*`])`
> Waits for child process *pid* to exit and returns its process ID. Waits for any child process if *pid*=0 is specified. Flags may be 0 or a logical or of the constants WNOHANG and WUNTRACE.

`waitpid2(`*`pid`*`[, `*`flags`*`])`
> Waits for child process *pid* to exit and returns its process ID and exit status as an array.

Constants

`PRIO_PROCESS`
> Process priority. Specified in a logical or as the third argument of the `setpriority` method.

`PRIO_PGRP`
> Process group priority. Specified in a logical or as the third argument of the `setpriority` method.

`PRIO_USER`
> User priority. Specified in a logical or as the third argument of the `setpriority` method.

`WNOHANG`
> Terminate immediately without blocking if no child has exited. Specified in a logical or as the second argument of the `waitpid` and `waitpid2` methods.

`WUNTRACED`
> Terminate any stopped children whose status has not been reported. Specified in a logical or as the second argument of the `waitpid` and `waitpid2` methods.

Threads

Threads are a powerful tool for creating and maintaining cleaner code, and in many implementations, for making your software more responsive. In Ruby, the former benefit is the one emphasized—cleaner code—since Ruby implements "microthreads." *Microthreads* are in-process threads simulated with `setjmp`/`longjmp` in the Ruby interpreter itself. Hence, Ruby's `Thread` class isn't dependent on the underlying threads library or operating systems, making Ruby more portable.

Thread

Thread class

The class for user-level threads. When the main thread terminates, the other threads are killed, and the interpreter quits.

Class Methods

`Thread::abort_on_exception`
> Returns `true` if thread is set to abort on an exception.

`Thread::abort_on_exception=bool`
> Sets whether or not to abort on an exception. When aborting on an exception, displays an error message for exceptions raised in the thread and quits the program.

`Thread::critical`
> Returns `true` when scheduling of existing threads is prohibited.

`Thread::critical=bool`
> Sets the status of thread-scheduling prohibition.

`Thread::current`
> Returns the current thread.

`Thread::exit`
> Terminates the current thread.

`Thread::fork([arg...]) {|x...|...}`
> See `Thread::start([arg...]) {|x...|...}`.

`Thread::kill(th)`
> Terminates the specified thread.

`Thread::list`
> Returns an array of all threads.

`Thread::main`
> Returns the main thread.

`Thread::new([arg...]) {|x...|...}`
> See `Thread::start([arg...]) {|x...|...}`.

`Thread::pass`
> Passes execution to another thread.

```
Thread::start([arg...]) {|x...|...}
Thread::fork([arg...]) {|x...|...}
Thread::new([arg...]) {|x...|...}
```
Creates a new thread and executes the block in it. Arguments are passed directly to the block.

`Thread::stop`
Stops the current thread.

Instance Methods

`t[name]`
Retrieves the value of a thread-local variable associated with *name*. The *name* is either a string or a symbol.

`t[name]=value`
Sets the *value* of a thread-local variable.

`t.abort_on_exception`
Returns `true` if thread is set to abort on an exception.

`t.abort_on_exception=bool`
Sets whether or not this thread will abort on an exception. When aborting on an exception, displays an error message for exceptions raised in the thread and quits the program.

`t.alive?`
Returns `true` if the thread is alive (sleeping or running).

`t.exit`
See *t.kill*.

`t.join`
Waits for the thread to terminate. If the thread is terminated with an exception, that exception is raised again.

`t.key?(name)`
Returns `true` if a thread-local variable associated with *name* exists.

`t.kill`
`t.exit`
Terminates the thread.

`t.raise(exc[, mesg])`
Raises an exception from the thread.

`t.run`
Makes the thread eligible for scheduling and invokes the scheduler.

`t.safe_level`
Returns the value of `$SAFE`, the thread's safe level.

`t.status`
Returns the status of thread (`true` if alive, `false` if terminated normally, and `nil` if terminated with an exception).

`t.stop?`
Returns `true` if the thread is stopped.

`t.value`

Waits for the thread to terminate and returns the value of the last expression evaluated. If the thread is terminated with an exception, that exception is raised again.

`t.wakeup`

Marks the thread as eligible for scheduling.

ThreadGroup Thread group class

A thread can belong to only one thread group at a time. Until a change of group is specified, a newly created thread belongs to the same thread group as the thread that originally created it.

Class Method

`ThreadGroup::new`

Creates a new thread group.

Instance Methods

`tg.add(th)`

Adds *th* to the thread group. A thread can belong to only one group at a time.

`tg.list`

Returns an array of threads belonging to the thread group.

Constants

`Default`

The default thread group.

Exceptions

Ruby's exception handling class, **Exception**, and its descendents provide support for the notion that the code discovering some sort of error condition may not be the same code that can handle that error condition.

Exception Superclass for exceptions

Instance Methods

`e.backtrace`

Returns backtrace information (from where exception occurred) as an array of strings.

`e.exception`

Returns clone of the exception object *e*. This method is used by **raise** method.

`e.message`

Returns exception message.

Errno

`Errno::ENOENT` and other errors are defined in this module.

Built-in Exceptions

`Exception` and the classes derived from it provide a variety of fundamental building blocks for handling error conditions in your Ruby scripts. Of course with the power you know and love from OOP, you can easily extend and adapt these basic classes as you see fit.

The following are abstract `Exception` classes:

`Exception`
> Superclass of all exceptions

`ScriptError`
> Error originating from program mistakes

`StandardError`
> Superclass of standard error exceptions; caught if no class is specified by rescue

The following are subclasses of `StandardError`:

`ArgumentError`
> Argument error (incorrect number of arguments, etc.)

`EOFError`
> End of file reached

`FloatDomainError`
> Float calculation error

`IndexError`
> Error related to index.

`IOError`
> Error related to input or output.

`LocalJumpError`
> Error related to break, next, redo, retry, or return from wrong place.

`NoMemoryError`
> Insufficient memory.

`RangeError`
> Error produced when range exceeded

`RegexpError`
> Regular expression error

`RuntimeError`
> General runtime error

`SecurityError`
> Error related to security

SystemCallError
   Superclass of system call exceptions

SystemStackError
   Insufficient stack area

TypeError
   Error produced when types don't match

ZeroDivisionError
   Error produced when attempting to divide by zero

The following are two subclasses of SystemCallError. See <sys/errno.h> for details.

Errno::ENOENT
   File or directory doesn't exist

Errno::EPERM
   Insufficient access rights

The following are subclasses of ScriptError:

LoadError
   Error occurring during the loading of libraries

NameError
   Name error caused by accessing undefined name, etc.

NotImplementedError
   Function not supported by interpreter called

SyntaxError
   Error related to syntax

The following are subclasses of Exception:

Fatal
   Fatal error that can't ever be caught

Interrupt
   Interrupt (SIGINT) received

SystemExit
   exit called

Classes and Modules

Support for OOP in Ruby can be found in the Ruby classes Class and Module. All class objects are of class Class, and the Module class provides support for namespaces and mix-ins.

Module   Module class

A Module is similar to a class, except that it has no superclass and can't be instantiated.

Class Methods

Module::class_variables

    Returns an array of class variable names.

Module::constants

    Returns an array of constant names.

Module::nesting

    Returns an array of classes and modules nested at the point of call.

Module::new

    Creates a new anonymous module.

Instance Methods

m < mod

    Returns `true` if *m* is a descendant of *mod*.

m <= mod

    Returns `true` if *m* is a descendant of or equal to *mod*.

m <=> mod

    Returns +1 if *m* is an ancestor of *mod*, 0 if *m* is the same as *mod*, and -1 if *m* is a descendant of *mod*.

m === obj

    Returns `true` if *obj* is an instance of *m* or one of its descendants.

m > mod

    Returns `true` if *m* is an ancestor of *mod*.

m >= mod

    Returns `true` if *m* is an ancestor of or equal to *mod*.

m.ancestors

    Returns an array of ancestors, including both classes and modules.

m.const_defined?(*name*)

    Returns `true` if the constant specified by *name* is defined.

m.const_get(*name*)

    Returns the value of the specified constant.

m.const_set(*name*, *value*)

    Sets the *value* of a constant.

m.constants

    Returns an array of constant names.

m.included_modules

    Returns an array of names of included modules.

m.instance_method(*name*)

    Returns a `UnboundMethod` object corresponding to *name*. An exception is raised if the corresponding method doesn't exist. `UnboundMethod` should be bound before invocation.

```
unbound_plus = Fixnum.instance_method(:+)
plus = unbound_plus.bind(1)
p plus.call(2)          # => 3  (1+2)
```

`m.instance_methods([all=false])`

>Returns an array of instance method names. If *all* is `true`, instance methods from superclasses are also returned.

`m.method_defined?(name)`

>Returns `true` if the method specified by *name* is defined *m*.

`m.module_eval(str)`
`m.module_eval {...}`

>Evaluates *str* or block in the context of *m*. If a method is defined, that method is added to *m*.

`m.name`

>Returns the module's name.

`m.private_class_method(name...)`

>Sets visibility of class methods to `private`. *name* can be either a symbol or string.

`m.private_instance_methods([all=false])`

>Returns an array of instance methods whose visibility is private. If *all* is `true`, instance methods from superclasses are also returned.

`m.protected_instance_methods([all=false])`

>Returns an array of instance methods whose visibility is protected. If *all* is `true`, instance methods from superclasses are also returned.

`m.public_class_method(name...)`

>Sets visibility of class methods to `public`. *name* can be either a symbol or string.

`m.public_instance_methods([all=false])`

>Returns an array of instance methods whose visibility is public. If *all* is `true`, instance methods from superclasses are also returned.

Private Instance Methods

`alias_method(new, old)`

>Creates an alias for a method. Equivalent to the `alias` statement except that the name is specified with a symbol or string.

`append_features(mod)`

>Adds module definitions (methods and constants) of *mod* to the current module. This is the callback method used by `include`. Can be redefined for callback processing during the inclusion of modules. Used as a hook.

`attr(name[, flag=false])`

>Defines a named attribute, creating a method, *name*, for accessing the instance variable *@name*. If *flag* is `true`, also defines a writable method *name=* for setting the attribute.

`attr_accessor(name...)`

>Defines read accessor (*name*) and write accessor (*name=*) for each instance variable *@name*.

`attr_reader(name...)`

>Defines read accessor (*name*) for each instance variable *@name*.

`attr_writer(`*name...*`)`

Defines write accessor (*name=*) for each instance variable *@name*.

`extend_object(`*obj*`)`

Adds the current module's methods and constants to *obj*. This is the callback method used by `Object#extend`. Used as a hook.

`include(`*mod...*`)`

Includes the methods and constants of *mod*.

`method_added(`*name*`)`

Method called by the interpreter every time a method is defined with the `def` statement. The standard definition does nothing. Used as a callback.

`module_function(`*name...*`)`

Copies the definition of each of the instance methods specified by *name* as a class method and converts it to a module function.

`private([`*name...*`])`

Sets the visibility of each instance method specified by *name* to `private`. If used with no arguments, sets the visibility of subsequently defined methods to `private`.

`protected([`*name...*`])`

Sets the visibility of each instance method specified by *name* to be protected. If used with no arguments, sets the visibility of subsequently defined methods to be protected.

`public([`*name...*`])`

Sets the visibility of each instance method specified by *name* to public. If used with no arguments, sets the visibility of subsequently defined methods to public.

`remove_const(`*name*`)`

Removes the definition of constant, *name*.

`remove_method(`*name*`)`

Removes method (*name*) from the current class. If a method of the same name is defined in a superclass, it becomes visible.

```
class Foo
    def foo
      puts "Foo"
    end
end

class Bar<Foo
    def foo
      puts "Bar"
    end
end

b = Bar.new
b.foo
class Bar
```

```
        remove method ·foo
    end
    b.foo
```

undef_method(*name*)

Turns method (*name*) into an undefined method. Even if a method of the same name is defined in a superclass, it becomes invisible to that class or module.

```
class Foo
    def foo
    end
end

class Bar<Foo
  undef_method :foo
end

b = Bar.new
b.foo
```

Class

A class named **Class** is a class for every class of Ruby :-). This means classes are first-class objects in Ruby. **Class** can be created by a **class** statement. In addition, even unnamed classes can be created by **Class::new**.

Inherited Class

Module

Inherited Class

Object

Class Methods

Class::inherited(*c*)

Called when a subclass is defined. Used as a callback.

Class::new([*superclass*=Object])

Creates a new class.

Instance Methods

Class class doesn't inherit the **module_function** method.

***c*.class_eval**

Alias for ***c*.module_eval**.

***c*.name**

Returns the class name.

```
c.new([arg...])
```
　　Creates an instance of the class. Any arguments or blocks get passed directly
　　to the initialize method of the object created.

```
c.superclass
```
　　Returns the class's superclass.

Proc Objects and Bindings

The Proc class provides support for converting blocks into objects and manipulating them just like other objects in Ruby. The nice thing is that the Proc object
you create can recreate its execution environment when you need to call it. Ruby
also provides you with a tool for packaging up an execution environment for use
later, via the Binding class.

Proc
Procedure object class

Proc is an objectified block that is given to a method. You can create a Proc
object by calling the proc method or by using the block argument of the method.

```
p1 = proc{|a| a + 1}    # Proc from a block
p2 = proc                # Proc from a block given to this method

def foo(&proc)           # Proc from a block given to this method
  proc.call(42)          # invoke Proc, equivalent to yield
end
```
```
Proc::new
Proc::new {|x|...}
```
　　Converts the block into a Proc object. If a block isn't passed, the block asso-
　　ciated with the calling method is converted into a Proc object. Equivalent to
　　built-in functions lambda and proc.

Instance Methods

```
p[arg...]
p.call([arg...])
```
　　Calls a Proc object.

```
p.arity
```
　　Returns the number of arguments accepted by a Proc object p. For p that
　　take a variable number of arguments, returns –n–1, where n is the number of
　　mandatory arguments. Notice {|a|} gives –1, since it works like {|*a|}
　　when multiple arguments are passed.

```
Proc.new{||}.arity        #=> 0
Proc.new{|a|}.arity       #=> -1
Proc.new{|a,b|}.arity     #=> 2
Proc.new{|a,b,c|}.arity   #=> 3
Proc.new{|*a|}.arity      #=> -1
Proc.new{|a,*b|}.arity    #=> -2
```

Method   Method object class

The method of an object that has been made into an object in its own right. Created using the method *obj*.method(*name*).

Instance Methods

m[*arg*...]
m.arity

> Returns the number of arguments accepted by *m*. For methods that take a variable number of arguments, returns −n−1, where n is the number of least required arguments.

m.call([*arg*...])

> Calls a method object.

m.to_proc

> Converts *m* into a Proc object.

m.unbind

> Returns an UnboundMethod object corresponding to *m*.

Built-ins

UnboundMethod   Method without receiver bind class

The method definition without a receiver relationship. You can't invoke UnboundMethod. You have to bind UnboundMethod to get a callable Method object. Created using the method Module#instance_method(name) or Method#unbind.

Inherited Class

Method

Instance Method

um.bind(*obj*)

> Returns callable Method object bound to *obj*. *obj* must be an instance of the class from which *UnboundMethod* retrieved.

```
unbound_plus = String.instance_method(:+)
plus = unbound_plus.bind("a")    # bind it first
p plus.call("b")                 # => "ab" ("a"+"b")
unbound_plus.bind(1)             # error! 1 is not a String.
```

Binding   Encapsulated execution context class

An object encapsulating the execution context (variables, methods, self, blocks, etc.) at some place in the code. Created using the built-in function binding. Used as the second argument of the built-in function eval. See eval in the previous section.

Continuation

Allows a return to (continuation of) execution from a certain place in the code. Created using the built-in function `callcc`. See `callcc` in the previous section.

Instance Method

`c.call([arg...])`
> Continues execution from the end of the `callcc` block that created the Continuation. `callcc` returns *arg*..., or `nil` if no arguments are specified.

Miscellaneous Classes and Modules

Of course, there's a whole lot of other stuff that you need in just about every Ruby program: things like garbage collection (GC module), Truth (via **TrueClass** and **FalseClass**), the ability to poke around at the objects inside a running Ruby script (via **ObjectSpace**), and so on. There's nothing here that you won't find consistent with Ruby's philosophy of transparency, so dive right in.

GC

GC module is a collection of garbage collection related operations.

Module Methods

`disable`
> Disables GC

`enable`
> Enables GC

`start`
> Starts GC

Instance Method

`g.garbage_collect`
> Starts GC

ObjectSpace

ObjectSpace module provides manipulation on collection of existing objects.

Module Functions

`_id2ref(id)`
> Obtains object from *id*. Do not use this method (intended for internal use only), especially in finalizers. *id* is already made unavailable when finalizers are called.

`define_finalizer(obj, proc)`
`define_finalizer(obj) {|id|...}`
> Creates a finalizer for *obj*. *obj* should not be referenced directly nor indirectly from the finalizers.

```
class Foo
def Foo::finalizer(io)     # typical idiom for finalizers
io.close
end
def initialize(path)
@io = open(path)
ObjectSpace.define_finalizer(self, Foo::finalizer(@io))
end
```
each_object([c]) {|x|...}

Calls the block once for all objects. When c is specified, executes the block once for all objects that match c or are subclasses of c (for which kind_of?(c) is true).

garbage_collect

Starts GC. Alias for GC::start.

undefine_finalizer(*obj*)

Removes all finalizers for *obj*.

NilClass   Nil class

The only instance of NilClass is nil. NilClass has no special methods of its own.

TrueClass   True class

The only instance of TrueClass is true. TrueClass provides a few logical operations, which evaluate both operands before executing the methods, unlike && or || operators.

Instance Methods

true & *other*

Logical AND, without short circuit behavior

true | *other*

Logical OR, without short circuit behavior

true ^ *other*

Logical exclusive Or (XOR)

FalseClass   False class

The only instance of FalseClass is false. FalseClass provides a few logical operations, which do evaluate both operands before, unlike && or || operators.

Instance Methods

false & *other*

Logical AND, without short circuit behavior

false | *other*

Logical OR, without short circuit behavior

false ^ *other*
> Exclusive Or (XOR)

Data
C data wrapper class

Data is an external language data wrapper used by extension libraries. It has no special methods of its own.

Marshal
Object storage module

Marshal is a module for dumping objects to and loading them from a file or string.

Module Functions

dump(*obj*[, *port*][, *level*])
> Dumps an object. Dumps to port if an IO object is specified as *port*. If *port* isn't specified, *obj* is returned as a dumped string. If *level* is specified, subobjects up to that depth are dumped.

load(*from*)
restore(*from*)
> Restores a dumped object. The string or IO object dumped to is specified in *from*.

Range
Range class

Range is a class for interval. Ranges can be created using .. or ... operators or using the Range::new method.

Included Module

Enumerable

Class Method

Range::new(*first*, *last*[, *excl*=false])
> Creates a Range object. Does not include the end value if *excl* is true. *first* and *last* should be comparable using <=> and should have succ method.

Instance Methods

r === *other*
> Returns true if *other* is within the range.

r.begin
r.first
> Returns the first object in the range.

r.each { |*x*| ... }
> Executes the block for each object within the range.
> ```
> (1..5).each {|x|
>   puts x        # prints 1 to 5
> ```

---

104   Chapter 3 – Built-in Library Reference

```
            }
        (1...5).each {|x|
        puts x          # prints 1 to 4
        }
```
r.end
r.last
> Returns the last object in the range.

r.size
r.length
> Returns the number of objects in the range. If the range is specified by some-
> thing other than an integer, the number of objects is counted using the each
> method.

Struct

Structure class

Stuct is a abstract class that collects named attributes bundled in an object. You
have to generate your own Struct class (subclass of Struct) using
Struct::new, which returns new Struct class.

Example
```
S = Struct::new(:foo, :bar)
s = S::new(1,2)
s.foo           # => 1
s.bar = 5       # update the member
s.bar           # => 5
s               # => #<S foo=1, bar=5>
```

Included Module

Enumerable

Class Method

Struct::new([*name*,] *mem*...)
> Creates a new structure class containing members specified by *mem*... . If
> *name* is given, the structure class is bound to the constant under Struct, for
> example Struct::Passwd. Note that Struct::new doesn't return a struc-
> ture object itself, but rather a class that is used as a template for creating each
> structure.

Structure Class Methods

S::members
> Returns an array of member names.

S::new(*value*...)
> Creates a new structure object. *value* objects specify the initial value of each
> member and must match the number of members specified when the struc-
> ture was created.

Instance Methods

s[*mem*]

Returns the value of member *mem* where *mem* is a symbol or integer. If *mem* is an integer, the value of the *mem*th member is returned.

s[*mem*]=*value*

Sets the value of member *mem*. *mem* may be a symbol or integer.

s.each {|*x*|...}

Calls block once for each member.

s.members

Returns an array of member names.

s.values

Returns an array containing the value of each member.

Time
Time class

Time is an object corresponding to a certain time. Internally, it's stored as a number of seconds since the *epoch*, 00:00:00, January 1, 1970 UTC. Time class can handle both a system's local time and UTC at the same time, but no other time zones can be handled.

Included Module

Comparable

Class Methods

Time::at(*time*[, *usec*=0])

Creates a Time object. time may be a Time object or an integer representing the number of seconds elapsed since the epoch, 00:00:00, January 1, 1970 UTC.

Time::gm(*year*[,*month*=1[,*day*=1[,*hour*=0[,*min*=0[,*sec*=0[,*usec*=0]]]]]])

see Time::utc(year[,month=1[,day=1[,hour=0[,min=0[,sec=0 [,usec=]]]]]])

Time::local(*year*[,*month*=1[,*day*=1[,*hour*=0[,*min*=0[,*sec*=0 [,*usec*=0]]]]]])

Time::mktime(*year*[,*month*=1[,*day*=1[,*hour*=0[,*min*=0[,*sec*=0 [,*usec*=0]]]]]])

Creates a Time object interpreted in the local time zone.

Time::new

Time::now

Creates a Time object expressing the current system time.

Time::times

Returns a Tms structure containing user and system CPU times retrieved by the times system call. Here are the Tms structure members:

utime

>User CPU time

stime

>System CPU time

cutime

>CPU time elapsed for user child processes

cstime

>CPU time elapsed for system child processes

Time::utc(*year*[,*month*=1[,*day*=1[,*hour*=0[,*min*=0[,*sec*=0
[,*usec*=0]]]]]])

Time::gm(*year*[,*month*=1[,*day*=1[,*hour*=0[,*min*=0[,*sec*=0[,*usec*=0]]]]]])

>Creates a **Time** object interpreted as UTC (Coordinated Universal Time, formally known as GMT).

Instance Methods

t + n

>Returns a **Time** object with *n* number of seconds added.

t - x

>If *x* is another **Time** object, the time difference is returned in seconds as a **Float**. If *x* is a number, a **Time** object with *x* number of seconds subtracted is returned.

t <=> other
t > other
t >= other
t < other
t <= other

>Time comparisons.

t.asctime
t.ctime

>Returns *t* as a string.

t.day
t.mday

>Returns the day of the month (1–31) for *t*.

t.gmtime

>See *t.utc*

t.gmtime?

>See *t.utc?*

t.hour

>Returns the hour of the day (0–23) for *t*.

t.isdst

>Returns **true** if *t* occurs during daylight saving time.

t.localtime

>Turns on representation mode of *t* to local time.

`t.min`
> Returns the minute of the hour (1–59) for `t`.

`t.mon`
`t.month`
> Returns the month of the year (1–12) for `t`.

`t.sec`
> Returns the second of the minute (1–60) for `t`. There can be a 60th second of the minute due to leap second.

`t.strftime(`*`format`*`)`
> Formats `t` according to formatting directives, which may be any of these:

%A	Full weekday name (Sunday, Monday...)
%a	Abbreviated weekday name (Sun, Mon...)
%B	Full month name (January, February...)
%b	Abbreviated month name (Jan, Feb...)
%c	Date and time
%d	Day of the month in decimal (01–31)
%H	Hour, 24-hour clock (00–23)
%I	Hour, 12-hour clock (01–12)
%j	Day of the year (001–366)
%M	Minutes (00–59)
%m	Month in decimal (01–12)
%p	Meridian indicator (A.M. or P.M.)
%S	Seconds (00–60)
%U	Week number, with the first Sunday as the first day of the first week (00–53)
%W	Week number, with the first Monday as the first day of the first week (00–53)
%w	Day of the week, Sunday being 0 (0–6)
%X	Time only
%x	Date only
%Y	Year with century
%y	Year without century (00–99)
%Z	Time zone
%%	Literal % character

`t.to_f`
> Returns the value of `t` as a **Float** of seconds since the epoch, including microseconds.

`t.to_i`
`t.tv_sec`
> Returns the value of `t` as an integer number of seconds since the epoch.

`t.tv_usec`
`t.usec`
> Returns just the number of microseconds of `t`.

`t.utc`
`t.gmtime`

Converts *t* to UTC, modifying the receiver.

`t.utc?`
`t.gmt?`

Returns true if *t* represents a time in UTC.

`t.wday`

Returns the day of the week (0–6, Sunday being 0) for *t*.

`t.yday`

Returns the day of the year (1–366) for *t*.

`t.year`

Returns the year for *t*.

`t.zone`

Returns the local time zone for *t*.

CHAPTER 4

Standard Library Reference

We will now explore the useful libraries that come with the standard Ruby distribution, from network access via HTTP and CGI programming to data persistence using the DBM library.

Standard Library

The Ruby standard library extends the foundation of the Ruby built-in library with classes and abstractions for a variety of programming needs, including network programming, operating-system services, threads, and more. These classes provide flexible capabilities at a high level of abstraction, giving you the ability to create powerful Ruby scripts useful in a variety of problem domains.

Many common tasks are performed by Ruby programmers all over the world. Some of these tasks include network access such as TCP/IP and CGI, OS access, database access, controlling processes with threads, numeric calculations, implementing design classes, and manipulating dates. These are used so frequently that they are included with all standard distributions of Ruby; when you access these classes and methods from your programs, they will be available from the Standard Library. Could you write these libraries yourself? Probably. Would you feel confident they have been exhaustively tested, optimized, and debugged? Usually not. The Standard Library is a great time saver. And as Ruby grows and evolves, so will its Standard Library, to everyone's benefit.

Although not every library section will contain all these entries, the basic format for each section is as follows:

*   Required library
*   Example
*   Inherited class

110

- Class methods
- Instance methods

Network

Use Ruby's network classes to let your scripts speak basic protocols such as TCP and UDP as a client, a server, or both. These libraries provide socket access to a variety of Internet protocols and classes that make access to those protocols easier. You can even crawl up the protocol stack and find support for higher-level protocols like FTP, HTTP, IMAP, and so on. All have an intuitive, transparent interface that won't get in your way. This is the largest group of libraries and one of the most frequently used.

Oh, and don't worry. There's support for doing web programming through the CGI, `CGI::Cookie` and `CGI::Session` classes.

BasicSocket   Socket-related superclass

`BasicSocket` is an abstract base class for network socket-related classes. This class provides common behavior among `Socket` classes.

Required Library

`require 'socket'`

Inherited Class

`IO`

Class Methods

`BasicSocket::do_not_reverse_lookup`
> Returns `true` if a query returns numeric address, not hostname

`BasicSocket::do_not_reverse_lookup=bool`
> Sets `reverse_lookup` status

Instance Methods

`s.getpeername`
> Returns information on this connection's peer socket as a `struct sockaddr` packed into a string.

`s.getsockname`
> Returns information on `s` as a `struct sockaddr` packed into a string.

`s.getsockopt(lev, optname)`
> Gets the specified socket option.

`s.setsockopt(lev, optname, value)`
> Sets the specified socket option.

`s.shutdown([how=2])`
> Shuts down the socket connection. 0 shuts down receiving, 1 sending, and 2 both.

`s.recv(len[, flags])`
> Receives data from *s*, and returns it as a string.

`s.send(mesg, flags[, to])`
> Sends data over the socket *s*, returning the length of the data sent. *to* may be a `struct sockaddr` packed into a string indicating the recipient address.

IPSocket   IP socket class

IPSocket class is a base class of `TCPSocket` and `UDPSocket`. `IPSocket` class provides common behavior among Internet Protocol (IP) sockets. Sockets classes in Ruby support IPv6, if the native platform supports it.

Required Library

`require 'socket'`

Inherited Class

`BasicSocket`

Class Method

`IPSocket::getaddress(host)`
> Returns the IP address of the specified *host*. The IP address is returned as a string such as `127.10.0.1` (IPv4) or `::1` (IPv6).

Instance Methods

`s.addr`
> Returns an array containing information on the socket connection (`AF_INET`, port, hostname, and IP address)
>
> ```
> s = TCPSocket.open("www.ruby-lang.org", "http")
> s.addr# => ["AF_INET", 4030, "dhcp198.priv.netlab.jp",
>     "192.168.1.198"]
> ```

`s.peeraddr`
> Returns an array containing information on the peer socket in the same format as *s*.`addr`
>
> ```
> s = TCPSocket.open("www.ruby-lang.org", "daytime")
> s.recvfrom(255)
> # => ["Wed Aug  1 00:30:54 2001\r\n", ["AF_INET", 13, "www",
>     "210.251.121.214"]]
> ```

`s.recvfrom(len[, flags])`
> Receives data and returns it in an array that also includes information on the sender's socket in the same format as *s*.`addr`

UDPSocket   UDP socket class

`UDPSocket` is a class for User Datagram Protocol (UDP), which is a connection-less, unreliable protocol.

Instance Method

s.accept

> Waits for a connection and returns a new TCPSocket object once one is accepted

---

UNIXSocket   Unix domain socket class

UNIXSocket is a class for the Unix domain, which can be specified by the path.

Required Library

require 'socket'

Inherited Class

BasicSocket

Class Methods

UNIXSocket::new(*path*)
UNIXSocket::open(*path*)

> Creates a Unix domain socket

Instance Methods

s.addr

> Returns an array containing information on the socket (AF_UNIX and the path)

s.path

> Returns the path of the Unix domain socket

s.peeraddr

> Returns an array containing information on the peer socket in the same format as s.addr

s.recvfrom(*len*[, *flag*=0])

> Receives data and returns it in an array that also includes information on the sender's socket in the same format as s.addr

---

UNIXServer   Unix domain server socket class

UNIXServer is a class for server-side Unix domain sockets. A UNIXServer waits for client connection by the accept method, then returns a UNIXSocket object connected to the client.

Required Library

require 'socket'

Inherited Class

UNIXSocket

Class Methods

```
UNIXServer::new(path)
UNIXServer::open(path)
```
    Creates a server socket

Instance Method

`s.accept`
    Waits for a connection and returns a new `UNIXSocket` object once one is accepted

---

Socket
General socket class

The `Socket` class is necessary to gain access to all the operating system's socket interfaces. Interface structures can be created using `String#pack`.

Required Library

`require 'socket'`

Inherited Class

`BasicSocket`

Class Methods

`Socket::for_fd(fd)`
    Creates a socket object corresponding to the file descriptor *fd* (an integer).

`Socket::getaddrinfo(host, port[, family[, type[, proto[, flags]]]])`
    Returns an array containing socket address information (address family, port number, hostname, host IP address, protocol family, socket type, and protocol).

```
Socket::getaddrinfo("www.ruby-lang.org", "echo", Socket::AF_INET,
Socket::SOCK_DGRAM)
# => [["AF_INET", 7, "www", "210.251.121.214", 2, 2, 17]]
```

`Socket::gethostbyaddr(addr[, type=Socket::AF_INET)`
    Returns an array containing socket address information (address family, port number, hostname, host IP address, protocol family, socket type, and protocol).

```
Socket::getaddrinfo("www.ruby-lang.org", "echo", Socket::AF_INET,
Socket::SOCK_DGRAM)
# => [["AF_INET", 7, "www", "210.251.121.214", 2, 2, 17]]
```

`Socket::gethostbyname(name)`
    Returns an array containing host information retrieved from a host *name*.

```
Socket.gethostbyaddr(([127,0,0,1].pack("CCCC")))
# => ["ev", ["localhost", "ev.netlab.jp"], 2, "\177\000\000\001"]
```

`Socket::gethostname`
    Returns the current hostname.

Socket..getnameinfo(*addr*[, *flags*])

Returns an array containing the name of the host and service retrieved from the specified socket address information. addr may be a struct sockaddr packed into a string or an array (address family, port, and hostname).

```
sockaddr = [Socket::AF_INET, 80, 127,0,0,1,""].pack("snCCCCa8")
Socket::getnameinfo(sockaddr)                      # => ["ev","www"]

Socket::getnameinfo(["AF_INET",80,"localhost"]) # => ["ev","www"]
```

Socket::getservbyname(*service*[, *proto*="tcp"])

Returns the port number for *service* and *proto* specified.

```
Socket::getservbyname("http") # => 80
```

Socket::new(domain, type, proto)
Socket::open(domain, type, proto)

Creates a socket.

Socket::socketpair(*domain, type, proto*)
Socket::pair(*domain, type, proto*)

Returns an array containing a pair of connected sockets.

Instance Methods

s.accept

Waits for a connection and, once one is accepted, returns a new socket object in an array that also includes a struct sockaddr packed into a string.

s.addr

Synonym for *s*.getsockname. Returns struct socaddr packed in a string.

s.bind(*addr*)

Binds *s* to addr, a sockaddr structure packed into a string.

s.connect(*addr*)

Connects *s* to addr, a sockaddr structure packed into a string.

s.listen(*backlog*)

Specifies the size of the *backlog* queue.

s.recvfrom(*len*[, *flags*])

Receives data and returns it in an array that also includes information on the sender's socket in the form of a sockaddr structure packed into a string.

s.peeraddr

Synonym for *s*.getpeername. Returns struct socaddr packed in a string.

Constants

The following constants are defined for use in socket specifications:

```
AF_INET
AF_UNIX
MSG_OOB
MSG_PEEK
SOCK_DGRAM
SOCK_STREAM
SOL_SOCKET
```

```
SO_KEEPALIVE
SO_LINGER
SO_SNDBUF
. . .
```

These constants are also defined in the module `Socket::Constants` and are used by including them in your code.

Net::FTP   FTP connection class

`Net::FTP` is a class for File Transfer Protocol (FTP) client-side connection.

Required Library

`require 'net/ftp'`

Example

```
require 'net/ftp'

ftp = Net::FTP::new("ftp.ruby-lang.org")
ftp.login("anonymous", "matz@ruby-lang.org")
ftp.chdir("/pub/ruby")
tgz = ftp.list("ruby-*.tar.gz").sort.last
print "the latest version is ", tgz, "\n"
ftp.getbinaryfile(tgz, tgz)
ftp.close
```

Class Methods

`Net::FTP::new([host[, user[, passwd[, acct]]]])`
`Net::FTP::open(host[, user[, passwd[, acct]]])`
    Creates a `Net::FTP` object

Instance Methods

`f.abort`
    Aborts the previous command.

`f.acct(acct)`
    Sets the account.

`f.chdir(path)`
    Changes the current directory.

`f.close`
    Closes the connection.

`f.closed?`
    Returns `true` if the connection is closed.

`f.connect(host[, port=21])`
    Connects to host.

`f.debug_mode`
    Returns the debug mode status.

`f.debug_mode=bool`
    Sets the debug mode status.

---

f.delete(*file*)
> Deletes a file.

f.getbinaryfile(*remote, local*[, *blocksize*=4096[, *callback*]])
f.getbinaryfile(*remote, local*[, *blocksize*=4096]) {|*data*|...}
f.gettextfile(*remote, local*[, *callback*])
f.gettextfile(*remote, local*) {|*data*|...}
> Retrieves a remote file from the server. If callback or a block is specified, it's executed with the retrieved data. gettextfile performs newline code conversion.

f.help([*arg*])
> Displays help.

f.lastresp
> Returns the server's last response.

f.list(*path...*)
f.dir(*path...*)
f.ls(*path...*)
> Returns an array of file information in the directory. If a block is specified, it iterates through the listing.
>
>   f.list("/pub/ruby") # =>
>   ["drwxr-xr-x   2 matz   users   4096 Jul 17 1998 1.0",...]

f.login([*user*="anonymous"[, *passwd*[, *acct*]]])
> Logs into the server.

f.mkdir(*path*)
> Creates a directory.

f.mtime(*file*[, *local*=false])
> Returns the last modification time of *file*. If *local* is true, it's returned as a local time, otherwise as Coordinated Universal Time (UTC) time.

f.nlst([*dir*])
> Returns an array of filenames in the directory.
>
>   f.nlst("/pub/ruby") # => ["/pub/ruby/1.0",...]

f.putbinaryfile(*local, remote*[, *blocksize*=4096[, *callback*]])
f.putbinaryfile(*local, remote*[, *blocksize*=4096]) {|*data*|...}
f.puttextfile(*local, remote*[, *callback*])
f.puttextfile(*local, remote*) {|*data*|...}
> Transfers a file. If callback or a block is specified, the data is passed to it and is run. puttextfile performs newline code conversion.

f.pwd
f.getdir
> Returns the current directory.

f.passive
> Returns true if passive mode is enabled.

f.passive=*bool*
> Sets passive mode on or off.

f.quit
> Exits the FTP session.

f.rename(*old*, *new*)
> Renames filename *old* to *new*.

f.rmdir(*path*)
> Removes the directory specified by *path*.

f.resume
> Returns true if resumption of file transfers is enabled.

f.resume=*bool*
> Sets file transfer resumption on or off.

f.return_code
> Returns the newline code of the current session.

f.return_code=*ret*
> Sets the newline code of the current session.

f.size(*file*)
> Returns the size of file.

f.status
> Returns the status.

f.system
> Returns system information.

f.welcome
> Returns the server's welcome message.

Net::HTTP HTTP connection class

Net::HTTP is a class for Hypertext Transfer Protocol (HTTP) client-side connection.

Required Library

require 'net/http'

Example

```
require 'net/http'

h = Net::HTTP::new("www.ruby-lang.org")
resp, data = h.get("/en/index.html")
print data
```

Class Methods

```
Net::HTTP::new([host="localhost"[,port=80[,proxy[, proxy_
   port]]]])
Net::HTTP::start([host="localhost"[,port=80[,proxy[, proxy_
   port]]]])
Net::HTTP::start([host="localhost"[,port=80[,proxy[, proxy_
   port]]]]) {|http|...}
```

Creates a Net::HTTP connection object. If a block is specified, the block is executed with the Net::HTTP object passed as an parameter. The connection is closed automatically when the block exits.

Instance Methods

h.finish

Closes the HTTP session.

```
h.get(path[, header[, dest]])
h.get(path[, header]) {|str|...}
```

Retrieves data from *path* using a GET request, and returns an array containing an HTTPResponse object and the data. *header* may be a hash indicating header names and values. *dest* may be a string to which the data is appended. If a block is specified, the retrieved data is passed to it.

h.head(path[, header])

Sends a HEAD request for *path*, and returns the response.

```
h.post(path, data[, header[, dest]])
h.post(path, data[, header]) {|str|...}
```

Sends *data* to *path* using a POST request, and returns an array containing an HTTPResponse object and the reply body. Although the post method's HTTP request type is different, the block and arguments, such as *header* and *dest*, are handled in the same way as *h*.get.

```
h.start
h.start {|http|...}
```

Starts an HTTP session. If a block is specified, the session is terminated when the block exits.

Net::IMAP   IMAP access class

Net::IMAP is a class for Internet Message Access Protocol Version 4 (IMAP4) client-side connection. IMAP4 allows you to store and manage messages in the server side.

Required Library

require "net/imap"

Example

```
require "net/imap"
imap = Net::IMAP::new("imap.ruby-lang.org")
  imap.login("matz", "skwkgjv;")
  imap.select("inbox")
```

```
fetch_result = imap.fetch(1..-1, "UID")
search_result = imap.search(["BODY", "hello"])
imap.disconnect
```

Class Methods

Net::IMAP::add_authenticator(*auth_type*, *authenticator*)
> Adds an authenticator for Net::IMAP#authenticate.

Net::IMAP::debug
> Returns true if in the debug mode.

Net::IMAP::debug=*bool*
> Sets the debug mode.

Net::IMAP::new(*host*[, *port*=143])
> Creates a new Net::IMAP object and connects it to the specified *port* on the named *host*.

Instance Methods

imap.append(*mailbox*, *message*[, *flags* [, *date_time*]])
> Appends the *message* to the end of the *mailbox*.

```
imap.append("inbox", <<EOF.gsub(/\n/, "\r\n"), [:Seen], Time.now)
Subject: hello
From: shugo@ruby-lang.org
To: shugo@ruby-lang.org

hello world
EOF
```

imap.authenticate(*auth_type*, *arg*...)
> Authenticates the client. The *auth_type* parameter is a string that represents the authentication mechanism to be used. Currently Net::IMAP supports "LOGIN" and "CRAM-MD5" for the *auth_type*.

```
imap.authenticate('CRAM-MD5', "matz", "crampass")
```

imap.capability
> Returns an array of capabilities that the server supports.

```
imap.capability  # => ["IMAP4", "IMAP4REV1", "NAMESPACE", ...]
```

imap.check
> Requests a checkpoint of the current mailbox.

imap.close
> Closes the current mailbox. Also permanently removes from the mailbox all messages that have the \Deleted flag set.

imap.copy(*mesgs*, *mailbox*)
> Copies *mesgs* in the current mailbox to the end of the specified *mailbox*. *mesgs* is an array of message sequence numbers or a Range object.

imap.create(*mailbox*)
> Creates a new *mailbox*.

imap.delete(*mailbox*)
> Removes the *mailbox*.

imap.disconnect

> Disconnects from the server.

imap.examine(*mailbox*)

> Selects a *mailbox* as a current mailbox so that messages in the mailbox can be accessed. The selected mailbox is identified as read-only.

imap.expunge

> Removes from the current mailbox all messages that have \Deleted flag set.

imap.fetch(*mesgs, attr*)

> Fetches data associated with a message in the mailbox. *mesgs* is an array of message sequence numbers or an Range object. The return_value is an array of Net::IMAP::FetchData.

```
data = imap.uid_fetch(98, ["RFC822.SIZE", "INTERNALDATE"])[0]
data.seqno                    #=> 6
data.attr["RFC822.SIZE"]      #=> 611
data.attr["INTERNALDATE"]     #=> "12-Oct-2000 22:40:59 +0900"
data.attr["UID"]              #=> 98
```

imap.greeting

> Returns an initial greeting response from the server.

imap.list(*dir, pattern*)

> Returns an array of mailbox information in *dir* matching *pattern*. The return value is an array of Net::IMAP::MailboxList. *pattern* may contain wildcards * (which matches any characters) and % (which matches any characters except delimiter).

```
imap.list("foo", "*")# matches any mailbox under foo recursively
imap.list("foo", "f%")
                    # matches any mailbox start with "f" under "foo"
```

imap.login(*user, password*)

> Logs into the server.

imap.logout

> Logs out from the server.

imap.lsub(*refname, mailbox*)

> Returns an array of subscribed mailbox information in *dir* matching *pattern*. The return value is an array of Net::IMAP::MailboxList. *pattern* may contain wildcards * (which matches any characters) and % (which matches any characters except delimiter).

imap.noop

> Sends a NOOP command to the server. It does nothing.

imap.rename(*mailbox, newname*)

> Renames the *mailbox* to *newname*.

imap.responses

> Returns recorded untagged responses.

```
imap.select("inbox")
imap.responses["EXISTS"][-1]        #=> 2
imap.responses["UIDVALIDITY"][-1]   #=> 968263756
```

imap.search(*keys*[, *charset*])

>   Searches the mailbox for messages that match the given searching criteria, and
>   returns an array of message sequence numbers.

```
imap.search(["SUBJECT", "hello"])     #=> [1, 6, 7, 8]
imap.search('SUBJECT "hello"')        #=> [1, 6, 7, 8]
```

imap.select(*mailbox*)

>   Selects a *mailbox* as a current mailbox so that messages in the mailbox can
>   be accessed.

imap.sort(*sort_keys*, *search_keys*, *charset*)

>   Returns an array of message sequence numbers that matches *search_keys*
>   sorted according to the *sort_keys*.

```
imap.sort(["FROM"], ["ALL"], "US-ASCII")
                                  #=> [1, 2, 3, 5, 6, 7, 8, 4, 9]
imap.sort(["DATE"], ["SUBJECT", "hello"], "US-ASCII")
                                  #=> [6, 7, 8, 1]
```

imap.status(*mailbox*, *attr*)

>   Returns the status of the *mailbox*. The return value is a hash of attributes.

```
imap.status("inbox", ["MESSAGES", "RECENT"]) #=>
    {"RECENT"=>0, "MESSAGES"=>44}
```

imap.store(*mesgs*, *attr*, flags)

>   Stores data associated with a message in the mailbox. *mesgs* is an array of
>   message sequence numbers or a Range object.

```
# add \Deleted to FLAGS attribute to mails No.6,7,8.
imap.store(6..8, "+FLAGS", [:Deleted])
```

imap.subscribe(*mailbox*)

>   Appends the specified *mailbox* to the list of active or subscribed mailboxes.

imap.unsubscribe(*mailbox*)

>   Removes the specified *mailbox* from the list of active or subscribed
>   mailboxes.

imap.uid_copy(*mesg*, *mailbox*)

>   Copies *mesgs* in the current mailbox to the end of the specified *mailbox*.
>   *mesgs* is an array of unique message identifiers or a Range_object.

imap.uid_fetch(*mesgs*, *attr*)

>   Fetches data associated with a message in the current mailbox. *mesgs* is an
>   array of unique message identifiers or an Range object. The return value is an
>   array of Net::IMAP::FetchData.

imap.uid_search(*keys*[, *charset*])

>   Searches the mailbox for messages that match the given search criteria, and
>   returns an array of unique identifiers.

imap.uid_sort(*sort_keys*, *search_keys*, *charset*)

>   Returns an array of unique message identifiers that matches *search_keys*
>   sorted according to the *sort_keys*.

```
imap.uid_store(mesgs, attr, flags)
```
Stores data associated with a message in the mailbox. *mesgs* is an array of unique message identifiers or a Range object. The return value is an array of Net::IMAP::FetchData.

Net::POP3

Net::POP3 is a class for Post Office Protocol Version 3 (POP3) client-side connection. POP3 is a simple protocol that retrieves incoming mail from the server.

Required Library

```
require 'net/pop'
```

Example

```
require 'net/pop'

pop = Net::POP3::new("pop.ruby-lang.org")
# authenticate just for SMTP before POP
pop.start("matz", "skwkgjv;") {
  mails = pop.mails          # array of Net::POPMail
}
```

Class Methods

```
Net::POP3::new([addr="localhost"[, port=80]])
```
Creates a new Net::POP3 object.

```
Net::POP3::start([addr="localhost"[, port=80[, ...]]])
Net::POP3::start([addr="localhost"[,port=80[,...]]]) {|pop|...}
```
Equivalent to Net::POP3::new(*addr*, *port*).start(...). A newly created Net::POP3 object is passed to the block, if specified. The POP3 session is terminated when the block exits.

Instance Methods

```
p.each {|mail|...}
```
Synonym for *p*.mails.each.

```
p.finish
```
Closes the POP3 session.

```
p.mails
```
Returns an array of Net::POPMail objects.

```
p.start(acct, passwd)
p.start(acct, passwd) {|pop|...}
```
Starts a POP3 session. If a block is specified, the session is terminated when the block exits.

Net::APOP

The Net::APOP class has the same interface as Net::POP3. They differ only in their method of authentication.

Required Library

require 'net/pop'

Inherited Class

Net::POP3

Net::POPMail   POP mail class

The Net::POPMail class is used by classes Net::POP3 and Net::APOP to return individual message objects.

Required Library

require 'net/pop'

Instance Methods

m.all([*dest*])
m.mail([*dest*])
m.pop([*dest*])
> Retrieves the contents of mail messages. If *dest* is specified, each message is appended to it using the << method. If a block is specified, it's passed the contents of each message as a string and run once for each line in the message.

m.delete
> Deletes the message.

m.deleted?
> Returns true if the message has been deleted.

m.header([*dest*])
> Returns the message header.

m.size
> Returns the message size in bytes.

m.top(*lineno*[, *dest*])
> Returns the message header and *lineno* number of lines of the body.

Net::SMTP   SMTP connection class

Net::SMTP is a class for Simple Mail Transfer Protocol (SMTP) client-side connection. SMTP is a protocol to talk to Mail Transfer Agent (MTA).

Required Library

require 'net/smtp'

Example

```
require 'net/smtp'

user = "you@your-domain.com"
from = "matz@ruby-lang.org"
server = "localhost"
```

```
smtp = Net::SMTP::new(server)
smtp.start
smtp.sendmail(<<BODY, from, user)
From: matz@ruby-lang.org
Subject: this is a test mail.

this is body
BODY
smtp.finish
```

Class Methods

Net::SMTP::new([*addr*="localhost"[, *port*=25]])
> Creates a new Net::SMTP object.

Net::SMTP::start([*addr*="localhost"[,*port*=25[,...]]])
Net::SMTP::start([*addr*="localhost"[,*port*=25[,...]]]) {|*smtp*|...}
> Equivalent to Net::SMTP::new(*addr*, *port*).start(...). A newly created
> Net::SMTP object is passed to the block, if specified. The SMTP session is
> terminated when the block exits.

Instance Methods

s.finish
> Closes an SMTP session.

s.ready(*from*, *to*) {|*adapter*|...}
> Sends a message, passing an *adapter* object to the block. The message is
> sent by calling the adapter's write method.

s.start([*domain*[, *account*[, *password*[, *authtype*]]]])
s.start([*domain*[, *account*[, *password*[, *authtype*]]]]) {|*smtp*|...}
> Starts an SMTP session. An Net::SMTP object is passed to the block, if speci-
> fied. The session is terminated when the block exits.

s.send_mail(*mailsrc*, *from*, *to*)
s.sendmail(*mailsrc*, *from*, *to*)
> Sends mail. *to* may be either a string or an array of strings.

Net::Telnet   Telnet connection class

Net::Telnet is a class for a Telnet connection. This class isn't only a Telnet
protocol client but also a useful tool to interact with interactive services.

When a block is specified with class and instance methods of the Net::Telnet
class, it's passed status output strings from the server as they are received by the
method.

Required Library

require 'net/telnet'

Class Method

Net::Telnet::new(options)

Creates a `Net::Telnet` object. *options* may be a hash specifying zero or more of the following options:

Key	Function	Default
Binmode	Binary mode	false
Host	Telnet server	"localhost"
Output_log	Output log	nil (no output)
Dump_log	Dump log	nil (no output)
Port	Port to connect to	23
Prompt	Pattern matching the server's prompt	/[$%#>] \z/n
Telnetmode	Telnet mode	true
Timeout	Timeout	10
Waittime	Wait time	0
Proxy	Proxy	nil

Instance Methods

Besides the following methods, the `Net::Telnet` object delegates its methods to `Socket` object, so that methods provided by the `Socket` class (and its parent classes) are also available for `Net::Telnet`.

t.binmode
> Returns `true` if binary mode is enabled.

t.binmode=*bool*
> Sets binary mode on or off.

t.cmd(*options*)
> Sends a command to the server. *options* may be the command string to be sent to the server or a hash specifying one or more of the following options:

Key	Function	Default value
String	String to be sent	(Required)
Match	Pattern to match	Value of Prompt option
Timeout	Timeout	Value of Timeout option

t.login(*options*)
t.login(*user*[, *passwd*])
> Logs in to the server. The following hash options may be specified.:

Key	Function
Name	Username
Password	Password

t.print(*str*)
> Sends *str* to the server, performing Telnet protocol translation.

t.telnetmode
> Returns `true` if Telnet mode is enabled.

t.telnetmode=*bool*
> Sets Telnet mode on or off.

t.waitfor(*options*)

Waits for a response from the server. The same hash options may specified as with *t*.cmd.

t.write(*str*)

Sends *str* to the server without performing Telnet protocol translation.

CGI

CGI provides useful features to implement Common Gateway Interface (CGI) programs, such as retrieving CGI data from server, manipulating cookies, and generating the HTTP header and the HTML body.

Example

```
require 'cgi'

cgi = CGI::new("html3")

input, = cgi["input"]
if input
  input = CGI::unescape(input)
end
p input

begin
  value = Thread::new{
    $SAFE=4
    eval input
  }.value.inspect
rescue SecurityError
  value = "Sorry, you can't do this"
end

cgi.out {
  cgi.html{
    cgi.head{cgi.title{"Walter's Web Arithmetic Page"}} +
    cgi.body{
      cgi.form("post", "/cgi-bin/arith.rb") {
        "input your favorite expression: " +
        cgi.text_field("input", input) +
        cgi.br +
        "the result of you input: " +
        CGI::escapeHTML(value) +
        cgi.br +
        cgi.submit
      }
    }
  }
}
```

Required Library

```
require 'cgi'
```

Class Methods

`CGI::new([level="query"])`

Creates a CGI object. *level* may be one of the following options. If one of the HTML levels is specified, the following methods are defined for generating output conforming to that level:

query
> No HTML output generated

html3
> HTML3.2

html4
> HTML4.0 Strict

html4Tr
> HTML4.0 Transitional

html4Fr
> HTML4.0 Frameset

`CGI::escape(str)`

Escapes an unsafe string using URL-encoding.

`CGI::unescape(str)`

Expands a string that has been escaped using URL-encoding.

`CGI::escapeHTML(str)`

Escapes HTML special characters, including: & < >.

`CGI::unescapeHTML(str)`

Expands escaped HTML special characters, including: & < >.

`CGI::escapeElement(str[, element...])`

Escapes HTML special characters in the specified HTML elements.

`CGI::unescapeElement(str, element[, element...])`

Expands escaped HTML special characters in the specified HTML elements.

`CGI::parse(query)`

Parses the query and returns a hash containing its key-value pairs.

`CGI::pretty(string[, leader=" "])`

Returns a neatly formatted version of the HTML string. If *leader* is specified, it's written at the beginning of each line. The default value for *leader* is two spaces.

`CGI::rfc1123_date(time)`

Formats the data and time according to RFC-1123 (for example, Sat, 1 Jan 2000 00:00:00 GMT).

Instance Methods

`c[name]`

Returns an array containing the value of the field name corresponding to *name*.

`c.checkbox(`*name*`[,` *value*`[,` *check=false*`]])`
`c.checkbox(`*options*`)`
> Returns an HTML string defining a checkbox field. Tag attributes may be specified in a hash passed as an argument.

`c.checkbox_group(`*name*`,` *value...*`)`
`c.checkbox_group(`*options*`)`
> Returns an HTML string defining a checkbox group. Tag attributes may be specified in a hash passed as an argument.

`c.file_field(`*name*`[,` *size=20*`[,` *max*`]])`
`c.file_field(`*options*`)`
> Returns an HTML string defining a file field.

`c.form([`*method*`="post"[,` *url*`]]) {...}`
`c.form(`*options*`)`
> Returns an HTML string defining a form. If a block is specified, the string produced by its output creates the contents of the form. Tag attributes may be specified in a hash passed as an argument.

`c.cookies`
> Returns a hash containing a `CGI::Cookie` object containing keys and values from a cookie.

`c.header([`*header*`])`
> Returns a CGI header containing the information in *header*. If *header* is a hash, its key-value pairs are used to create the header.

`c.hidden(`*name*`[,` *value*`])`
`c.hidden(`*options*`)`
> Returns an HTML string defining a HIDDEN field. Tag attributes may be specified in a hash passed as an argument.

`c.image_button(`*url*`[,` *name*`[,` *alt*`]])`
`c.image_button(`*options*`)`
> Returns an HTML string defining an image button. Tag attributes may be specified in a hash passed as an argument.

`c.keys`
> Returns an array containing the field names from the form.

`c.key?(`*name*`)`
`c.has_key?(`*name*`)`
`c.include?(`*name*`)`
> Returns `true` if the form contains the specified field name.

`c.multipart_form([`*url*`[,` *encode*`]]) {...}`
`c.multipart_form(`*options*`) {...}`
> Returns an HTML string defining a multipart form. If a block is specified, the string produced by its output creates the contents of the form. Tag attributes may be specified in a hash passed as an argument.

`c.out([`*header*`]) {...}`
> Generates HTML output. Uses the string produced by the block's output to create the body of the page.

```
c.params
```
Returns a hash containing field names and values from the form.

```
c.params=hash
```
Sets field names and values in the form using a hash.

```
c.password_field(name[, value[, size=40[, max]]])
c.password_field(options)
```
Returns an HTML string defining a password field. Tag attributes may be specified in a hash passed as an argument.

```
c.popup_menu(name, value...)
c.popup_menu(options)
c.scrolling_list(name, value...)
c.scrolling_list(options)
```
Returns an HTML string defining a pop-up menu. Tag attributes may be specified in a hash passed as an argument.

```
c.radio_button(name[, value[, checked=false]])
c.radio_button(options)
```
Returns an HTML string defining a radio button. Tag attributes may be specified in a hash passed as an argument.

```
c.radio_group(name, value...)
c.radio_group(options)
```
Returns an HTML string defining a radio button group. Tag attributes may be specified in a hash passed as an argument.

```
c.reset(name[, value])
c.reset(options)
```
Returns an HTML string defining a reset button. Tag attributes may be specified in a hash passed as an argument.

```
c.text_field(name[, value[, size=40[, max]]])
c.text_field(options)
```
Returns an HTML string defining a text field. Tag attributes may be specified in a hash passed as an argument.

```
c.textarea(name[, cols=70[, rows=10]]) {...}
c.textarea(options) {...}
```
Returns an HTML string defining a text area. If a block is specified, the string produced by its output creates the contents of the text area. Tag attributes may be specified in a hash passed as an argument.

HTML Generation Methods

In addition to the previous instance methods, each CGI object provides the following methods, which generate HTML tag strings corresponding to the HTML level specified when the CGI object was created. These methods return a string that is produced by adding any specified tags to a body created from the string output of the block. Tag attributes may be specified in a hash that is passed as an argument to each method.

Here are the tags common to html3, html4, html4Tr, and html4Fr:

a	address	area	b	base
big	blockquote	body	br	caption
cite	code	dd	dfn	div
dl	doctype	dt	em	form
h1	h2	h3	h4	h5
h6	head	hr	html	i
img	input	kbd	li	link
map	meta	ol	option	p
param	pre	samp	script	select
small	strong	style	sub	submit
sup	table	td	th	title
tr	tt	ul	var	

Here are the html3 tags:

applet	basefont	center	dir	font
isindex	listing	menu	plaintext	strike
u	xmp			

Here are the html4 tags:

abbr	acronym	bdo	button	col
colgroup	del	fieldset	ins	label
legend	noscript	object	optgroup	q
span	tbody	tfoot	thead	

Here are the html4Tr tags:

abbr	acronym	applet	basefont	bdo
button	center	col	colgroup	del
dir	fieldset	font	iframe	ins
isindex	label	legend	map	menu
noframes	noscript	object	optgroup	q
s	span	strike	tbody	tfoot
thead	u			

Here are the htmlFr tags:

abbr	acronym	applet	basefont	bdo
button	center	col	colgroup	del
dir	fieldset	font	frame	frameset
iframe	ins	isindex	label	legend
menu	noframes	noscript	object	optgroup
q	s	span	strike	tbody
tfoot	thead	u		

Object Attributes

The CGI class has the following accessors:

accept	Acceptable MIME type
accept_charset	Acceptable character set
accept_encoding	Acceptable encoding
accept_language	Acceptable language
auth_type	Authentication type
raw_cookie	Cookie data (raw string)
content_length	Content length
content_type	Content type
From	Client email address
gateway_interface	CGI version string
path_info	Extra path
path_translated	Converted extra path
Query_string	Query string
referer	Previously accessed URL
remote_addr	Client host address
remote_host	Client hostname
remote_ident	Client name
remote_user	Authenticated user
request_method	Request method (GET, POST, etc.)
script_name	Program name
server_name	Server name
server_port	Server port
server_protocol	Server protocol
server_software	Server software
user_agent	User agent

CGI::Cookie   HTTP cookie class

CGI::Cookie represents the HTTP cookie that carries information between HTTP sessions.

Required Library

require 'cgi'

Object Attributes

The CGI::Cookie class has the following accessors:

c.name	Cookie name
c.value	An array of cookie values
c.path	The cookie's path
c.domain	The domain
c.expires	The expiration time (as a Time object)
c.secure	True if secure cookie

CGI::Session

CGI::Session maintains a persistent session between HTTP accesses. Session information is represented by string to string mapping. Session information can be stored via the user-defined database class.

Required Library

```
require 'cgi/session'
```

Example

```
request 'cgi/session'

cgi = CGI::new("html3")
s = CGI::Session(cgi)

if s["last_modified"]
  # previously saved data
  t = s["last_modified"].to_i
else
  t = Time.now.to_i
  # save data to session database
  s["last_modified"] = t.to_s
end
  # ... continues ...
```

Class Methods

CGI::Session::new(*cgi*[, *option*])

Starts a new CGI session and returns the corresponding CGI::Session object. *option* may be an option hash specifying one or more of the following:

Key	Function	Default value
session_key	Key name holding the session ID	_session_id
session_id	Unique session ID	Generated automatically
new_session	If true, a new session is created	false
database_manager	Database manager class for storing session data	CGI::Session::FileStore

An option hash can specify options when creating the database manager object. The default database manager class (CGI::Session::FileStore) recognizes the following options:

Key	Function	Default value
tmpdir	Directory for temporary files	/tmp
prefix	Prefix for temporary files	None

Methods for Database Manager

Database manager object should have following methods:

`initialize(`*session*`[, `*options*`])`
> Initializes the database. *session* is a `CGI::Session` object. *options* is an option hash that passed to `CGI::Session::new`

`restore`
> Returns the hash that contains session-specific data from the database

`update`
> Updates the hash returned by `restore`

`close`
> Closes the database

`delete`
> Removes the session-specific data from the database

Instance Methods

`s[key]`
> Returns the value for the specified session *key*

`s[key]=value`
> Sets the value for the specified session *key*

`s.delete`
> Deletes the session

`s.update`
> Writes session data to the database, calling the update method of the database manager object

Operating System Services

A mixed bag of OS services are provided in the Ruby standard library, including curses, filesystem searching and file handling, command-line argument processing, and others.

If you're coming from another scripting language background, these classes will have interfaces you'll find familiar and straightforward access to Unix services. No surprises, here.

Curses   Character-based interface module

The `Curses` module provides an interface to the character-based interface library called `curses`.

Required Library

`require 'curses'`

Module Functions

`addch(`*ch*`)`
> Outputs one character to the screen

---

addstr(str)
> Outputs *str* to the screen

beep
> Beeps the bell

cbreak
> Turns on **cbreak** mode

nocbreak
> Turns off **cbreak** mode

clear
> Clears the screen

close_screen
> Finalizes the **curses** system

cols
> Returns the screen width

crmode
> Alias to the **cbreak**

nocrmode
> Alias to the **nocbreak**

delch
> Deletes a character at the cursor position

deleteln
> Deletes a line at the cursor position

doupdate
> Updates the screen by queued changes

echo
> Turns on echo mode

noecho
> Turns off echo mode

flash
> Flashes the screen

getch
> Reads one character from the keyboard

getstr
> Reads a line of string from the keyboard

inch
> Reads a character at the cursor position

init_screen
> Initializes the **curses** system

insch(ch)
> Outputs one character before the cursor

lines
> Returns the screen height

`nl`
> Turns on newline mode, which translates the return key into newline (\n)

`nonl`
> Turns off newline mode

`raw`
> Turns on raw mode

`noraw`
> Turns off raw mode

`refresh`
> Refreshes the screen

`setpos(y, x)`
> Moves the cursor to the (y, x) position

`standout`
> Turns on `standout` (highlighting) mode

`standend`
> Turn off `standout` mode

`stdscr`
> Returns the reference to the standard `curses` screen object

`ungetch(ch)`
> Pushes ch back to input buffer

Curses::Window
Character-based window class

`Curses::Window` is a class for character-based windows implemented by the `curses` library.

Required Library
```
require "curses"
```

Class Method
`Curses::Window::new(h, w, y, x)`
> Creates a new `curses` window of size (h, w) at position (y, x).

Instance Methods
`w << str`
`w.addstr(str)`
> Outputs str to the screen.

`w.addch(ch)`
> Outputs one character to the screen.

`w.begx`
> Returns the window's beginning x position.

`w.begy`
> Returns the window's beginning y position.

*w.*box(*v*, *h*)

> Draws a box around the window. *v* is a character that draws a vertical side. *h* is a character that draws a horizontal side.

*w.*clear

> Clears the window.

*w.*close

> Closes the window.

*w.*curx

> Returns *x* position of the window's cursor.

*w.*cury

> Returns *y* position of the window's cursor.

*w.*delch

> Deletes a character at the window's cursor position.

*w.*deleteln

> Deletes a line at the window's cursor position.

*w.*getch

> Reads one character from the keyboard.

*w.*getstr

> Reads a line of string from the keyboard.

*w.*inch

> Reads a character at the window's cursor position.

*w.*insch(*ch*)

> Outputs one character before the window's cursor.

*w.*maxx

> Returns the window's *x* size.

*w.*maxy

> Returns the window's *y* size.

*w.*move(*y*, *x*)

> Moves the window to the position (*y*, *x*).

*w.*refresh

> Refreshes the window.

*w.*setpos(*y*, *x*)

> Moves the window's cursor to the position (*y*, *x*).

*w.*standend

> Turns on standout (highlighting) mode in the window.

*w.*standout

> Turns off standout mode in the window.

*w.*subwin(*h*, *w*, *y*, *x*)

> Creates a new curses subwindow of size (*h*, *w*) in the window at position (*y*, *x*).

Etc

The Etc module provides functions to retrieve user account-related data from files under */etc* directory. This module is Unix-dependent.

Required Library

```
require 'etc'
```

Example

```
require 'etc'

print "you must be ", Etc.getlogin, ".\n"
```

Module Functions

getlogin

> Returns login name of the user. If this fails, try getpwuid.

getpwnam(*name*)

> Searches in /etc/passwd file (or equivalent database), and returns password entry for the user *name*. See getpwnam(3) for details. The return value is a passwd structure, which includes the following members:

name	Username(string)
passwd	Encrypted password(string)
uid	User ID(integer)
gid	Group ID(integer)
gecos	Gecos field(string)
dir	Home directory(string)
shell	Login shell(string)
change	Password change time(integer)
quota	Quota value(integer)
age	Password age(integer)
class	User access class(string)
comment	Comment(string)
expire	Account expiration time(integer)

getpwuid([*uid*])

> Returns passwd entry for the specified *uid*. If *uid* is omitted, uses the value from getuid. See getpwuid(3) for details.

getgrgid(*gid*)

> Searches in /etc/group file (or equivalent database), and returns group entry for the *gid*. See getgrgid(3) for detail. The return value is a group structure, which includes the following members:

name	Group name(string)
passwd	Group password(string)
gid	Group ID(integer)
mem	Array of the group member names

getgrnam(*name*)

> Returns the group entry for the specified *name*. The return value is the group structure. See getgrnam(3) for details.

---

group

    Iterates over all **group** entries.

passwd

    Iterates over all **passwd** entries.

Fcntl

The **Fcntl** module provides constant definitions for **IO#fcntl**.

Required Library

```
require 'fcntl'
```

Constants

F_DUPFD	Duplicates file descriptor
F_GETFD	Reads the close-on-exec flag
F_SETFD	Sets the close-on-exec flags
F_GETFL	Reads the descriptor's flags
F_SETFL	Gets the descriptor's flags (O_APPEND, O_NONBLOCK, or O_ASYNC)
F_GETLK	Gets the flock structure
F_SETLK	Gets lock according to the lock structure (nonblocking)
F_SETLKW	Sets lock like **F_SETLK** (blocking)
F_RDLCK	Reads lock flag for flock structure
F_WRLCK	Writes lock flag for flock structure
F_UNLCK	Unlocks flag for flock structure
FD_CLOEXEC	Close-on-exec flag
O_CREAT	Creates file if it doesn't exist
O_EXCL	File shouldn't exist before creation
O_TRUNC	Truncates to *length* 0
O_APPEND	Appends mode
O_NONBLOCK	Nonblocking mode
O_NDELAY	Nonblocking mode
O_RDONLY	Read-only mode
O_RDWR	Read-write mode
O_WRONLY	Write-only mode

Standard Library

Find

The **Find** module provides a depth-first directory traversal.

Required Library

```
require 'etc'
```

Example

```
require 'find'

# prints all files with ".c" extension.
Find.find(".") {|f|
  puts f if /\.c$/ =~ f
}
```

Module Functions

find(*path...*) {|*f*| ...}
    Traverses directory tree giving each filename to the block

prune
    Terminates traversal down from the current directory

---

ftools
File utility library

ftools is a library that enhances file handling utility class methods of the `File` class.

Required Library

```
require 'ftools'
```

Class Methods

File::chmod(*mode, files...*[,*verbose*=false])
    ftools enhances `File::chmod` to take verbose arguments. If the last argument is `true`, prints log to `stderr`.

File::cmp(*path1*, *path2*[, *verbose*=false])
File::compare(*path1*, *path2*[, *verbose*=false])
    Compares two files and returns `true` if they have identical contents. If *verbose* is `true`, prints log to `stderr`.

File::cp(*path1*, *path2*[, *verbose*=false])
File::copy(*path1*, *path2*[, *verbose*=false])
    Copies a file at *path1* to *path2*. If *verbose* is `true`, prints operation log to `stderr`.

File::install(*path1*, *path2*[, *mode* [, *verbose*=false]])
    Copies a file at *path1* to *path2*. If *mode* is supplied, its file permission is set to *mode*. If file at *path2* exists, it's removed before copying. If *verbose* is `true`, prints operation log to `stderr`.

File::makedirs(*path...*[, *verbose*=false])
File::mkpath(*path...*[, *verbose*=false])
    Creates the specified directories. If any parent directories in *path* don't exist, it creates them as well. If the last argument is `true`, prints operation log to `stderr`.

File::move(*path1*, *path2*[, *verbose=false*])
File::mv(*path1*, *path2*[, *verbose=false*])
> Moves file from *path1* to *path2*. If the last argument is true, prints operation log to stderr.

File::rm_f(*path...*[, *verbose=false*])
File::safe_unlink(*path...*[, *verbose=false*])
> Removes files regardless of file-permission mode. If the last argument is true, prints operation log to stderr.

File::syscopy(*path1*, *path2*)
> Copies a file from *path1* to *path2* using IO#sysread and IO#syswrite. *syscopy* copies permissions of the file as well.

GetoptLong Command line option parser

The GetoptLong class parses command-line option arguments in a way similar to GNU getoptlong library.

Required Library

```
require 'gettextfile'
```

Example

```
require 'getoptlong'

opt = GetoptLong.new(
    ['--max-size', '-m', GetoptLong::REQUIRED_ARGUMENT],
    ['--quiet',    '-q', GetoptLong::NO_ARGUMENT],
    ['--help',          GetoptLong::NO_ARGUMENT],
    ['--version',       GetoptLong::NO_ARGUMENT])
opt.each_option do |name,arg|
   case name
   when '--max-size'
  printf "max-size is %d\n", arg
   when '--quiet'
  print "be quiet!\n"
   when '--help'
  print "help message here\n"
  exit
   when '--version'
  print "version 0.1\n"
  exit
   end
end
```

Inherited Class

Object

Class Method

GetoptLong::new(*option...*)
> Creates and returns a GetoptLong object. If *options* are given, they are passed to the set_options method.

Instance Methods

opt.each {|*optname, optarg*|...}
opt.each_option {|*optname, optarg*|...}
> Iterates over each command-line option. Option name and value are passed to the block.

opt.get
opt.get_option
> Retrieves an option from command-line arguments, and returns the name-value pair of option.

opt.error
opt.error?
> Returns type of the current error or nil if no error occurs.

opt.error_message
> Returns an error message of the current error or nil if no error occurs.

opt.ordering=*ordering*
> Sets option ordering. *ordering* is any of PERMUTE, REQUIRE_ORDER, or RETURN_IN_ORDER.

opt.ordering
> Returns current ordering.

opt.quiet=*bool*
> Sets status of quiet mode. In quiet mode, option parser doesn't output error messages to stdout on errors. The default value is false.

opt.quiet
opt.quiet?
> Returns current status of quiet mode.

opt.set_options(*option*...)
> Sets command-line options that your program accepts, specified by arrays of option names and option type constants.
>
> Option type is any of NO_ARGUMENT, REQUIRED_ARGUMENT, or OPTIONAL_ARGUMENT. You have to call set_options before invoking get, get_option, each, or each_option.

opt.terminate
> Terminates option processing. Raises RuntimeError exception if any errors occur before termination.

opt.terminated?
> Returns true if option processing is finished without causing errors, otherwise returns false.

Constants

Ordering specifiers
> PERMUTE
>
> REQUIRE_ORDER
>
> RETURN_IN_ORDER

    NO_ARGUMENT

    REQUIRED_ARGUMENT

    OPTIONAL_ARGUMENT

PTY Pseudo TTY access module

The PTY module executes commands as if their standard I/O is connected to *ttys*.

Required Library

```
require "pty"
```

Module Functions

getpty(*command*)
spawn(*command*)
> Reserves a PTY, executes *command* over the PTY, and returns an array of three elements (reading I/O, writing I/O, and the PID of the child process). With a block, the array is passed to the block as block parameters. SIGCHLD is captured while *command* is running.

protect_signal {...}
> Protects block execution from SIGCHLD signal exception. This is required to invoke other subprocesses while using any PTY.

reset_signal
> Disables to handle SIGCHLD while PTY subprocess is active.

Readline GNU readline library interface

The Readline module provides a interface to the GNU line editing library named readline.

Required Library

```
require 'readline'
```

Example

```
require 'readline'
include Readline
line = readline("Prompt> ", true)
```

Module Function

readline(*prompt, add_history*)
> Reads one line with line editing. If the add is true, the line is also added to the history.

Module Methods

Readline::completion_proc=*proc*
> Specifies Proc object to determine completion behavior. Takes input string, and returns completion candidates.

`Readline::completion_proc`
> Returns the completion `Proc` object.

`Readline::completion_case_fold=bool`
> Sets whether or not to ignore case on completion.

`Readline::completion_case_fold`
> Returns `true` if completion ignores case.

`Readline::completion_append_character=char`
> Specifies a character to be appended on completion. If empty string ("") or nil
> is specified, nothing is appended.

`Readline::completion_append_character`
> Returns a string containing a character to be appended on completion.
> Default is a space.

`Readline::vi_editing_mode`
> Specifies *vi* editing mode.

`Readline::emacs_editing_mode`
> Specifies Emacs editing mode.

Constant

`HISTORY`
> The history buffer; it behaves just like an array.

Tempfile
Temporary file class

Temporary files are always deleted when garbage collection is activated, and Ruby
terminates.

Required Library

`require 'tempfile'`

Example

```
require 'tempfile'
f = Tempfile.new("foo")
f.print("foo\n")
f.close
f.open
p f.gets      # => "foo\n"
f.close(true) # f will be automatically removed
```

Class Method

`Tempfile::new(basename[, tmpdir="/tmp"])`
> Opens a temporary file that includes *basename* as part of the filename in w+
> mode.

`t.open`

Reopens the temporary file, allowing its contents to be read from the beginning of the file.

`t.close([permanently=false])`

Closes the temporary file. If *permanently* is `true`, the file is also deleted.

`t.path`

Returns the path of the temporary file.

In addition to the previous methods, objects of class `Tempfile` also possess all instance methods of class `File`.

Win32API   Microsoft Windows API access class

Win32API represents functions in Windows DLLs.

Required Library

```
require 'Win32API'
```

Example

```
require 'Win32API'

getch = Win32API.new("crtdll", "_getch", [], 'L')
puts getch.Call.chr
```

Class Method

`Win32API::new(dll, proc, import, export)`

Returns the object representing the `Win32API` function specified by *proc* name in *dll*, which has the signature specified by *import* and *export*. *import* is an array of strings denoting types. *export* is a type specifying string. Type string is any of the following:

"n" Number

"l" Number

"i" Integer

"p" Pointer

"v" Void (export only)

Type strings are case-insensitive.

Instance Methods

`call([arg...])`
`Call([arg...])`

Invokes the `Win32API` function. Arguments must conform the signature specified by `Win32API::new`.

Threads

Threading classes in the Ruby standard library extend and enhance the built-in library support for parallel programming with support for condition variables, monitors and mutexes, queues and a handy-dandy thread termination watcher class.

ConditionVariable
Synchronization condition variable class

This class represents condition variables for synchronization between threads.

Required Library

```
require 'thread'
```

Class Method

`ConditionVariable::new`
> Creates a `ConditionVariable` object

Instance Methods

`c.broadcast`
> Wakes up all waiting queued threads

`c.signal`
> Wakes up the next thread in the queue

`c.wait(mutex)`
> Waits on `condition variable`

Monitor
Exclusive monitor section class

This class represents exclusive sections between threads.

Required Library

```
require 'monitor'
```

Included Module

`MonitorMixin`

Class Method

`Monitor::new`
> Creates a `Monitor` object

Instance Methods

`m.enter`
> Enters exclusive section.

`m.exit`
> Leaves exclusive section.

`m.owner`
> Returns the thread that owns the monitor.

```
m.synchronize{...}
```
Enters exclusive section and executes the block. Leaves the exclusive section automatically when the block exits.

```
m.try_enter
```
Attempts to enter exclusive section. Returns `false` if lock fails.

MonitorMixin   Exclusive monitor section mix-in module

Adds monitor functionality to an arbitrary object by mixing the modules with `include`.

Required Library

```
require 'monitor'
```

Instance Methods

```
m.mon_enter
```
Enters exclusive section.

```
m.mon_exit
```
Leaves exclusive section.

```
m.mon_owner
```
Returns the thread that owns the monitor.

```
m.mon_synchronize{...}
```
Enters exclusive section and executes the block. Leaves the exclusive section automatically when the block exits.

```
m.try_mon_enter
```
Attempts to enter exclusive section. Returns `false` if lock fails.

Mutex   Mutual exclusion class

This class represents mutually exclusive locks.

Required Library

```
require 'thread'
```

Class Method

```
Mutex::new
```
Creates a `Mutex` object

Instance Methods

```
m.lock
```
Locks the `Mutex` object *m*

```
m.locked?
```
Returns `true` if *m* is locked.

```
m.synchronize {...}
```
Locks *m* and runs the block, then releases the lock when the block exits.

`m.try_lock`
> Attempts to lock *m.* Returns `false` if lock fails.

`m.unlock`
> Releases lock on *m.*

Queue   Message queue class

This class provides the way to communicate data between threads.

Required Library

`require 'thread'`

Class Method
`Queue::new`
> Creates a `queue` object

Instance Methods
`q.empty?`
> Returns `true` if the queue is empty.

`q.num_waiting`
> Returns the number of threads waiting on the queue.

`q.pop([non_block=false])`
> Retrieves data from the queue. If the queue is empty, the calling thread is suspended until data is pushed onto the queue. If *non_block* is `true`, the thread isn't suspended, and an exception is raised.

`q.push(obj)`
`q.enq(obj)`
> Pushes *obj* to the queue.

`q.size`
`q.length`
> Returns the length of the queue.

SizedQueue   Fixed-length queue class

This class represents queues of specified size capacity. The **push** operation may be blocked if the capacity is full.

Required Library

`require 'thread'`

Inherited Class

Queue

Class Method
`SizedQueue::new(max)`
> Creates a fixed-length queue with a maximum size of *max*

`q.max`
> Returns the maximum size of the queue

`q.max=n`
> Sets the maximum length of the queue

ThreadsWait
Thread termination watcher class

This class watches termination of multiple threads.

Required Library

`require 'thwait'`

Class Methods

`ThreadsWait::all_waits(th,...)`
`ThreadsWait::all_waits(th...) {...}`
> Waits until all specified threads are terminated. If a block is supplied for the method, evaluates it for each thread termination.

`ThreadsWait.new(th...)`
> Creates a `ThreadsWait` object, specifying threads to wait.

Instance Methods

`th.threads`
> Lists threads to be synchronized

`th.empty?`
> Returns `true` if there is no thread to be synchronized.

`th.finished?`
> Returns `true` if there is any terminated thread.

`th.join(th...)`
> Waits for specified threads.

`th.join_nowait(th...)`
> Specifies threads to wait; non-blocking.

`th.next_wait`
> Waits until any specified thread is terminated.

`th.all_waits`
`th.all_waits{...}`
> Waits until all specified threads are terminated. If a block is supplied for the method, evaluates it for each thread termination.

Data Persistence

These libraries provide interfaces or hooks into databases via various implementations (OS, GNU, and public domain).

Ruby lets you store and retrieve "live" data and objects in the filesystem with tools you're probably used through the `DBM`, `GDBM`, `SDBM`, and `PStore` classes.

DBM

DBM implements a database with the same interface as a hash. Keys and values are limited to strings. Uses ndbm library included in operating systems.

Required Library

```
require 'dbm'
```

Included Module

```
Enumerable
```

Class Methods

```
DBM::open(path[, mode=0666])
DBM::new(path[, mode=0666])
```
    Opens a new DBM database. Access rights to the database are specified in *mode* as an integer.

Instance Methods

The DBM class has all the methods of the Hash class except for `default`, `default=`, `dup`, and `rehash`. DBM also has the `close` method, which isn't in Hash.

```
d.close
```
    Closes DBM database

GDBM

GNU implementation of DBM. Has the same interface as DBM.

Required Library

```
require 'gdbm'
```

Instance Methods

In addition to methods from the DBM class, the GDBM class has the `reorganize` method.

```
d.reorganize
```
    Reconfigures the database; shouldn't be used with great frequency

---

SDBM

Public domain implementation of DBM. Has the same interface as DBM. Runs almost anywhere but has inferior performance and data-size limitations compared to other DBMs.

Required Library

```
require 'sdbm'
```

PStore

PStore is a simple object-oriented database class that provides almost arbitrary data persistence (using Marshal) and transaction.

Required Library

```
require 'pstore'
```

Class Method

PStore::new(*path*)

Creates a database object. Data is stored in a file specified by *path*.

Instance Methods

p.transaction {|*ps*|...}

Starts a transaction (a series of database operations). Access to the contents of the database can be achieved only through this transaction method.

p[*name*]

Retrieves an object stored in the database under the key name.

p[*name*]=*obj*

Stores *obj* in the database under the key name. When the transaction is completed, all objects accessed reflexively by *obj* (see Marshal in the section "Built-in Library" in Chapter 3) are saved in a file.

p.root?(*name*)

Returns true if the key name exists in the database.

p.commit

Completes the transaction. When this method is called, the block passed to the transaction method is executed, and changes to the database are written to the database file.

p.abort

Aborts the transaction. When this method is called, the execution of the block passed to the transaction method is terminated, and changes made to database objects during the transaction aren't written to the database file.

Numbers

These libraries let you handle numeric calculations using advanced numbers such as Complex, Rational, and Matrix.

Complex

When this library is loaded with require, the ability of the Math module is expanded to handle complex numbers.

Required Library

```
require 'complex'
```

Inherited Class

```
Numeric
```

Class Methods

```
Complex(r [, i=0])
Complex::new(r [, i=0])
```
    Creates a complex number object. The former is recommended.

Instance Methods

`c.abs`
    Returns the absolute value of the complex number *c*.

`c.abs2`
    Returns the square of the absolute value of the complex number *c*.

`c.arg`
    Returns the argument of the complex number *c*.

`c.conjugate`
    Returns the `conjugate` of the complex number *c*.

`c.image`
    Returns the imaginary part of the complex number *c*. The `Complex` library adds the image method to the **Numeric** class.

`c.polar`
    Returns the array `arr[c.abs, c.arg]`.

`c.real`
    Returns the real part of the complex number *c*. The `Complex` library adds the real method to the **Numeric** class.

Rational
Rational number class

When this library is loaded with **require**, the `**` operator method of the **Integer** class can handle rational numbers, and the following methods are added to the **Integer** class:

`to_r`
    Converts a number to a rational number

`lcm`
    Returns the least common multiple

`gcd`
    Returns the greatest common divisor

Required Library

require 'rational'

Inherited Class

Numeric

Class Methods

Rational(*a*, *b*)
Rational::new(*a*, *b*)
> Creates a rational number object. The former, Rational(*a*,*b*), is recommended.

Matrix

Required Library

require 'matrix'

Class Methods

Matrix::[*row*...]
> Creates a matrix where *row* indicates each row of the matrix.
>
>   Matrix[[11, 12], [21, 22]]

Matrix::identity(*n*)
Matrix::unit(*n*)
Matrix::I(*n*)
> Creates an n-by-*n* unit matrix.

Matrix::columns(*columns*)
> Creates a new matrix using *columns* as sets of column vectors.
>
>   Matrix::columns([[11, 12], [21, 22]]) # => Matrix[[11, 21], [12, 22]]

Matrix::column_vector(*column*)
> Creates a 1-by-*n* matrix such that column vector is *column*.

Matrix::diagonal(*value*...)
> Creates a matrix where diagonal components are specified by *value*.
>
>   Matrix.diagonal(11, 22, 33) # => Matrix[[11, 0, 0],
>   [0, 22, 0], [0, 0, 33]]

Matrix::rows(*rows*[, *copy*=true])
> Creates a matrix where *rows* is an array of arrays that indicates rows of the matrix. If the optional argument *copy* is false, use the given arrays as the internal structure of the matrix without copying.
>
>   Matrix::rows([[11, 12], [21, 22]])

Matrix::row_vector(*row*)
> Creates an 1-by-*n* matrix such that the row vector is *row*.

`Matrix::scalar(n, value)`

Creates an *n*-by-*n* diagonal matrix such that the diagonal components are given by *value*.

```
Matrix::scalar(3,81)    # => Matrix[[81,0,0],[0,81,0],[0,0,81]]
```

`Matrix::zero(n)`

Creates an *n*-by-*n* zero matrix.

Instance Methods

`m[i,j]`

Returns (*i*, *j*) component.

`m * mtx`

Multiplication.

`m + mtx`

Addition.

`m- mtx`

Subtraction.

`m / mtx`

Returns *m* * *mtx*.inv.

`m ** n`

Power of *n* over matrix.

`m.collect{...}`
`m.map{...}`

Creates a matrix that is the result of iteration of the given block over all components of the matrix *m*.

`m.column(j)`

Returns the *j*-th column vector of the matrix *m*. When the block is supplied for the method, the block is iterated over all column vectors.

`m.column_size`

Returns the number of columns.

`m.column_vectors`

Returns array of column vectors of the matrix *m*.

`m.determinant`
`m.det`

Returns the determinant of the matrix *m*.

`m.inverse`
`m.inv`

Returns an inversed matrix of the matrix *m*.

`m.minor(from_row, row_size, from_col, col_size)`
`m.minor(from_row..to_row, from_col..to_col)`

Returns submatrix of the matrix *m*.

`m.rank`

Returns the rank of the matrix *m*.

```
m.row(i)
m.row(i) {...}
```
>Returns the *i*-th row vector of the matrix *m*. When the block is supplied for the method, the block is iterated over all row vectors.

```
m.row_size
```
>Returns the number of rows.

```
m.row_vectors
```
>Returns an array of row vectors of the matrix *m*.

```
m.regular?
```
>Returns true if *m* is a regular matrix.

```
m.singular?
```
>Returns true if *m* is a singular (i.e., nonregular) matrix.

```
m.square?
```
>Returns true if *m* is a square matrix.

```
m.trace
m.tr
```
>Returns the trace of the matrix *m*.

```
m.transpose
m.t
```
>Returns the transpose of the matrix *m*.

Design Patterns

Design patterns are a terrific way to get your job done without reinventing the wheel. Ruby provides support in the standard library for a small number of commonly used design patterns. This group of libraries provides advanced object-oriented programming techniques for delegators, forwardables, singletons, and observers.

Delegator   Delegator pattern superclass

Delegator is an abstract class for the Delegator design pattern. Delegation is actually achieved by creating a subclass of the Delegator class.

Required Library

```
require 'delegate'
```

Class Method

```
Delegator::new(obj)
```
>Creates a delegate object to which methods of *obj* are forwarded.

Instance Method

```
__getobj__
```
>Returns the object to which methods are forwarded. Needs to be redefined in the subclass.

SimpleDelegator   Simple concrete Delegator pattern class

This class allows for easy implementation of the Delegator design pattern.

Required Library

```
require 'delegate'
```

Inherited Class

```
Delegator
```

Class Method

```
SimpleDelegator::new(obj)
```
    Creates an object that forwards methods to *obj*

Instance Method

```
__setobj__
```
    Sets the object to which methods are forwarded

DelegatorClass   Class creation function for Delegator patterns

This function dynamically creates a class that delegates to other fixed classes.

Required Library

```
require 'delegate'
```

Function

```
DelegateClass(c)
```
    Creates a new class to which the methods of class *c* are forwarded

Method of Generated Class

```
D::new(obj)
```
    Creates a delegate object with *obj* as the object to which methods are
    forwarded

Forwardable   Module to add selected method delegations to a class

The `Forwardable` module provides more explicit method delegation. You can
specify method name and destination object explicitly.

Required Library

```
require "forwardable"
```

Example

```
class Foo
  extend Forwardable
  # ...
```

```
    def_delegators("@out", "printf", "print")
    def_delegators(:@in, :gets)
    def_delegator(:@contents, :[], "content_at")
  end
  f = Foo.new
  f.printf("hello world\n")     # forward to @out.printf
  f.gets                        # forward to @in.gets
  f.content_at(1)               # forward to @contents.[]
```

Instance Methods

f.def_delegator(*accessor, method*[, *alt=method*])
f.def_instance_delegator(*accessor, method*[, *alt=method*])
> Defines delegation from *method* to *accessor*. If *alt* is specified, *alt* method is called instead of *method*.

f.def_delegators(*accessor, method...*)
f.def_instance_delegators(*accessor, method...*)
> Defines delegation to *accessor* for each *method*.

SingleForwardable   Selective delegation module

The `SingleForwardable` module provides more explicit method delegation for a specific object.

Required Library

```
require 'forwardable'
```

Example

```
  require 'forwardable'

  # ...
  g = Goo.new
  g.extend SingleForwardable
  g.def_delegator("@out", :puts)
  g.puts("hello world")              # forward to @out.puts
```

Instance Methods

f.def_singleton_delegator(*accessor, method*[, *alt=method*])
f.def_delegator(*accessor, method*[, *alt=method*])
> Defines delegation from *method* to *accessor*. If *alt* is specified, *alt* method is called instead of *method*.

f.def_singleton_delegators(*accessor, method...*)
f.def_delegators(*accessor, method...*)
> Defines delegation to *accessor* for each *method*.

Singleton   Singleton pattern module

The `Singleton` module allows the implementation of the Singleton design pattern. By including the module, you can ensure that only one instance of a class is created.

Required Library

require 'singleton'

Class Method

instance
> Returns the only instance of the class. If an instance has already been created, it's reused. instance is a class method added to classes that include the Singleton module.

Observable

Observable pattern module

The Observable module allows the implementation of the Observer design pattern. Classes that include this module can notify multiple observers of changes in self. Any object can become an observer as long as it has the update method.

Required Library

require 'observer'

Instance Methods

o.add_observer(obj)
> Adds observer obj as an observer of o.

o.count_observers
> Returns the number of observers of o.

o.changed([state=true])
> Sets the changed state of o.

o.changed?
> Returns true if o has been changed.

o.delete_observer(obj)
> Removes observer obj as an observer of o.

o.delete_observers
> Removes all observers of o.

o.notify_observers([arg...])
> If o's changed state is true, invokes the update method of each observer, passing it the specified arguments.

Miscellaneous Libraries

It almost goes without saying, but there's always a bunch of stuff that doesn't quite fit into any category. Ruby's standard library is no exception. This group of libraries includes anything that isn't in one of the preceding groups.

In Ruby's standard library, you'll find classes providing abstractions for date manipulation, timeouts on long operations, and MD5 and SHA1 message digests.

Date

Date is a class to represent the calendar date. Date is based on the Julian day number, which is the number of days since midday, January 1st 4713 BC.

Currently we use the Gregorian calendar, but the Julian calendar was used prior to that time (before 1752 in England, for example). The calendar shift date is different in each country. Date class can handle both calendars and arbitrary shift dates.

There's no relation between Julian day number and Julian calendar; it's just coincidence.

Required Library

require 'date'

Example

```
require 'date'

# 3000 days after Ruby was born
puts Date::new(1993,2,24)+3000, "\n"   # 2001-05-13
```

Included Module

Comparable

Class Methods

Date::exist?(*year, month, day*[, *start*])
Date::exist3?(*year, month, day*[, *start*])
> Returns the Julian day number corresponding to the specified *year*, *month*, and *day* of year, if they are correct. If they aren't correct, returns nil.

Date::exist2?(*year, yday*[, *start*])
> Returns the Julian day number corresponding to the specified *year* and *day* of year, if they are correct. If they aren't correct, returns nil.

Date::existw?(*year, week, wday*[, *start*])
> Returns the Julian day number corresponding to the specified calendar week-based *year*, calendar *week*, and calendar *weekday*, if they are correct. If they aren't correct, returns nil.

Date::new(*year, month, day*[, *start*])
Date::new3(*year, month, day*[, *start*])
> Creates a Date object corresponding to the specified *year*, *month*, and *day* of the month.

Date::new1(*jd*[, *start*])
> Creates a Date object corresponding to the specified Julian day number.

Date::new2(*year, yday*[, *start*])
> Creates a Date object corresponding to the specified *year* and day of the year.

Date::neww(*year, week, wday*[, *start*])
> Creates a Date object corresponding to the specified calendar week-based *year*, calendar *week*, and calendar weekday.

`Date::today([start])`

Creates a `Date` object corresponding to today's date.

Instance Methods

`d << n`

Returns a `Date` object that is *n* months earlier than *d*.

`d >> n`

Returns a `Date` object that is *n* months later than *d*.

`d <=> x`

Compares dates. *x* may be a `Date` object or an integer (Julian day number).

`d + n`

Returns a `Date` object that is *n* days later than *d*.

`d - x`

Returns the difference in terms of days if *x* is another `Date` object. If *x* is an integer, returns a `Date` object that is *x* days earlier than *d*.

`d.cwday`

Returns the calendar weekday (1–7, Monday being 1) for *d*.

`d.cweek`

Returns the calendar week (1–53) for *d*.

`d.cwyear`

Returns the calendar week-based year for *d*.

`d.day`
`d.mday`

Returns the day of the month (1–31) for *d*.

`d.downto(min) {|date|...}`

Runs block on dates ranging from *d* down to *min*. Equivalent to *d*.step(*min*), –1) {|*date*|...}.

`d.jd`

Returns the Julian day number for *d*.

`d.leap?`

Returns `true` if *d* is a leap year.

`d.mjd`

Returns the modified Julian day number for *d*. Modified Julian day number is the number of days since midnight November 17, 1858.

`d.mon`
`d.month`

Returns the month (1–12) for *d*.

`d.newsg([start])`

Copies *d* to a new `Date` object and returns it after converting its cutover date to *start*.

`d.next`
`d.succ`

Returns a new `Date` object one day later than *d*.

d.sg

    Returns the Julian day number of the start of Gregorian dates for *d*.

d.step(*limit, step*) {|*date*|...}

    Runs block on `Date` objects from *d* to *limit* incrementing *step* number of days each time.

d.upto(*max*) {|*date*|...}

    Runs block on dates ranging from *d* up to *max*. Equivalent to `d.step(*max*,` `1) {|*date*|...}`.

d.wday

    Returns the day of the week for *d* (0–6, Sunday being 0).

d.yday

    Returns the day of the year for *d* (1–366).

d.year

    Returns the year for *d*.

Constants

MONTHNAMES

    An array of the names of the months of the year

DAYNAMES

    An array of the names of the days of the week (Sunday being the first element)

ITALY

    Gregorian calendar start day number in Italy

ENGLAND

    Gregorian calendar start day number in England

JULIAN

    Start specifier for Julian calendar

GREGORIAN

    Start specifier for Gregorian calendar

ParseDate   Date representation parser module

The `ParseDate` module parses strings that represent calendar dates in various formats.

Required Library

`require 'parsedate'`

Module Function

parsedate(*str*[, *cyear*=false])

    Parses a date and/or time expression within *str* and returns the parsed elements (year, month, day, hour, minute, second, time zone, and day of the week) as an array. Sunday is represented as 0 in the day-of-the-week element. `nil` is returned for elements that can't be parsed or have no corresponding string representation. If *cyear* is `true`, years with a value of 68 or less are

---

interpreted as being in the 2000s and years ranging from 69 to 99 are interpreted as being in the 1900s. In summary, beware of the Y2K69 problem!

```
p ParseDate::parsedate("Fri Aug  3 17:16:57 JST 2001")
# => [2001, 8, 3, 17, 16, 57, "JST", 5]
p ParseDate::parsedate("1993-02-24")
# => [1993, 2, 24, nil, nil, nil, nil, nil]
```

timeout   Time out a lengthy procedure

Times out a lengthy procedure or those that continue execution beyond a set duration.

Required Library

```
require 'timeout'
```

Function

timeout(*sec*) {...}
>   Executes the block and returns **true** if the block execution terminates successfully prior to elapsing of the timeout period, otherwise immediately terminates execution of the block and raises a **TimeoutError** exception.
>
>   ```
>   require 'timeout'
>   status = timeout(5) {
>     # something that may take time
>   }
>   ```

MD5   MD5 message digest class

The **MD5** class provides a one-way hash function from arbitrary text data by using the algorithm described in RFC-1321

Example

```
requires 'md5'

md5 = MD5::new("matz")
puts md5.hexdigest # prints: 3eb50a8d683006fdf941b9860798f9aa
```

Class Methods

MD5::new([*str*])
MD5::md5([*str*])
>   Creates a new **MD5** object. If a string argument is given, it's added to the object.

Instance Methods

md.clone
>   Copies the **MD5** object.

md.digest
>   Returns the **MD5** hash of the added strings as a string of 16 bytes.

`md.hexdigest`

Returns the MD5 hash of the added strings as a string of 32 hexadecimal digits.

`md.update(str)`

`md << str`

Updates the MD5 object with the string *str*. Repeated calls are equivalent to a single call with the concatenation of all the arguments, i.e., m.update(a); m.update(b) is equivalent to m.update(a+b), and m << a << b is equivalent to m << a+b.

SHA1

SHA1 message digest class

The SHA1 class provides a one-way hash function from arbitrary text data.

Class Methods

`SHA1::new([str])`

`SHA1::sha1([str])`

Creates a new SHA1 object. If a string argument is given, it's added to the object.

Instance Methods

`sh.clone`

Copies the SHA1 object.

`sh.digest`

Returns the SHA1 hash of the added strings as a string of 16 bytes.

`sh.hexdigest`

Returns the SHA1 hash of the added strings as a string of 32 hexadecimal digits.

`sh.update(str)`

`sh << str`

Updates the SHA1 object with the string *str*. Repeated calls are equivalent to a single call with the concatenation of all the arguments, i.e., m.update(a); m.update(b) is equivalent to m.update(a+b), and m << a << b is equivalent to m << a+b.

CHAPTER 5

Ruby Tools

As a matter of course in Ruby, you edit your Ruby program and then feed it to the interpreter. Theoretically, the editor and interpreter are all you need to program Ruby. But you can get help from other tools. In this chapter, you will find descriptions of tools to help Ruby programmers.

Standard Tools

The standard Ruby distribution contains useful tools along with the interpreter and standard libraries: debugger, profiler, irb (which is interactive ruby), and ruby-mode for Emacs. These tools help you debug and improve your Ruby programs.

Debugger

It doesn't matter how easy a language is to use, it usually contains some bugs if it is more than a few lines long. To help deal with bugs, the standard distribution of Ruby includes a debugger. In order to start the Ruby debugger, load the debug library using the command-line option -r debug. The debugger stops before the first line of executable code and asks for the input of user commands.

Here are the debugger commands:

b[reak] [<*file*|*class*>:]<*line*|*method*>
    Sets breakpoints

wat[ch] *expression*
    Sets watchpoints

b[reak]
    Displays breakpoints and watchpoints

del[ete] [*n*]
    Deletes breakpoints

disp[lay] *expression*
> Displays value of *expression*

undisp[lay] [*n*]
> Removes display of *n*

c[ont]
> Continues execution

s[tep] [*n*]
> Executes next *n* lines stepping into methods

n[ext] [*n*]
> Executes next *n* lines stepping over methods

w[here]
> Displays stack frame

f[rame]
> Synonym for where

l[ist][<-|*n-m*>]
> Displays source lines from *n* to *m*

up [*n*]
> Moves up *n* levels in the stack frame

down [*n*]
> Moves down *n* levels in the stack frame

fin[ish]
> Finishes execution of the current method

tr[ace] [on|off]
> Toggles trace mode on and off

q[uit]
> Exits debugger

v[ar] g[lobal]
> Displays global variables

v[ar] l[ocal]
> Displays local variables

v[ar] i[instance] *object*
> Displays instance variables of *object*

v[ar] c[onst] *object*
> Displays constants of object

m[ethod] i[instance] *object*
> Displays instance methods of *object*

m[ethod] *class*|*module*
> Displays instance methods of the *class* or *module*

th[read] l[ist]
> Displays threads

```
th[read] c[ur[rent]]
    Displays current thread

th[read] n
    Stops specified thread

th[read] stop n>
    Synonym for th[read] n

th[read] c[ur[rent]] n>
    Synonym for th[read] n

th[read] resume n>
    Resumes thread n

p expression
    Evaluates the expression

h[elp]
    Displays help message

<everything else>
    Evaluates the expression
```

The following is a sample session that shows the debugger's output when it executes the *Sieves of Eratosthenes* program (a famous algorithm to calculate prime numbers). The interface is designed similarly to that of **gdb**.

```
% ruby -r debug sieve.rb 100
Debug.rb
Emacs support available.

sieve.rb:2:max = Integer(ARGV.shift || 100)
(rdb:1) list
[-3, 6] in sieve.rb
    1
=> 2  max = Integer(ARGV.shift || 100)
    3  sieve = []
    4  for i in 2 .. max
    5    sieve[i] = i
    6  end
(rdb:1) list
[7, 16] in sieve.rb
    7
    8  for i in 2 .. Math.sqrt(max)
    9    next unless sieve[i]
    10   (i*i).step(max, i) do |j|
    11     sieve[j] = nil
    12   end
    13  end
    14 puts sieve.compact.join ", "
  (rdb:1) b 8
Set breakpoint 1 at sieve.rb:8
(rdb:1) c
Breakpoint 1, toplevel at sieve.rb:8
sieve.rb:8:for i in 2 .. Math.sqrt(max)
(rdb:1) p sieve
```

```
[nil, nil, 2, 3, 4, 5, 6, 7, 8, 9, 10, 11, 12, 13, 14, 15, 16, 17, 18,
19, 20, 21, 22, 23, 24, 25, 26, 27, 28, 29, 30, 31, 32, 33, 34, 35, 36,
37, 38, 39, 40, 41, 42, 43, 44, 45, 46, 47, 48, 49, 50, 51, 52, 53, 54,
55, 56, 57, 58, 59, 60, 61, 62, 63, 64, 65, 66, 67, 68, 69, 70, 71, 72,
73, 74, 75, 76, 77, 78, 79, 80, 81, 82, 83, 84, 85, 86, 87, 88, 89, 90,
91, 92, 93, 94, 95, 96, 97, 98, 99, 100]
(rdb:1) del 1
(rdb:1) b 14
Set breakpoint 2 at sieve.rb:14
(rdb:1) c
Breakpoint 2, toplevel at sieve.rb:14
sieve.rb:14:puts sieve.compact.join ", "
(rdb:1) p sieve
[nil, nil, 2, 3, nil, 5, nil, 7, nil, nil, nil, 11, nil, 13, nil, nil,
nil, 17, nil, 19, nil, nil, nil, 23, nil, nil, nil, nil, nil, 29, nil,
31, nil, nil, nil, nil, nil, 37, nil, nil, nil, 41, nil, 43, nil, nil,
nil, 47, nil, nil, nil, nil, nil, 53, nil, nil, nil, nil, nil, 59, nil,
61, nil, nil, nil, nil, nil, 67, nil, nil, nil, 71, nil, 73, nil, nil,
nil, nil, nil, 79, nil, nil, nil, 83, nil, nil, nil, nil, nil, 89, nil,
nil, nil, nil, nil, nil, nil, 97, nil, nil, nil]
(rdb:1) sieve.compact
[2, 3, 5, 7, 11, 13, 17, 19, 23, 29, 31, 37, 41, 43, 47, 53, 59, 61, 67,
71, 73, 79, 83, 89, 97]
(rdb:1) c
2, 3, 5, 7, 11, 13, 17, 19, 23, 29, 31, 37, 41, 43, 47, 53, 59, 61, 67,
71, 73, 79, 83, 89, 97
```

Profiler

In most cases, you can improve the performance of a slow program by removing
the bottleneck. The *profiler* is a tool that finds the bottleneck. In order to add
profiling to your Ruby program, you need to first load the Profile library using
the command-line option -r profile. Here is the sample output from profiled
execution. You can tell Object#fact method is a bottleneck.

```
% ruby -r profile sample/fact.rb 100
93326215443944152681699238856266700490715968264381621468592963895217599990
322991560894146397615651828625369792082722375825118521091686400000000000000
000000000000
```

% time	cumulative seconds	self seconds	calls	self ms/call	total ms/call	name
66.67	0.07	0.07	1	66.67	66.67	Object#fact
16.67	0.08	0.02	1	16.67	16.67	Bignum#to_s
0.00	0.08	0.00	5	0.00	0.00	Fixnum#*
0.00	0.08	0.00	2	0.00	8.33	IO#write
0.00	0.08	0.00	1	0.00	0.00	Fixnum#==
0.00	0.08	0.00	95	0.00	0.00	Bignum#*
0.00	0.08	0.00	1	0.00	0.00	Module#method_added
0.00	0.08	0.00	101	0.00	0.00	Fixnum#>
0.00	0.08	0.00	1	0.00	16.67	Kernel.print
0.00	0.08	0.00	1	0.00	0.00	String#to_i
0.00	0.08	0.00	1	0.00	0.00	Array#[]
0.00	0.08	0.00	100	0.00	0.00	Fixnum#-
0.00	0.08	0.00	1	0.00	100.00	#toplevel

Tools

Tracer

When you want to trace the entrance and exit of each method, **tracer** is the tool for you. In order to add method call/return tracing to your Ruby program, load the Tracer library using the command-line option -r tracer. Here is sample output from **tracer**:

```
% ruby -r tracer fact.rb 2
#0:fact.rb:1::-: def fact(n)
#0:fact.rb:1:Module:>: def fact(n)
#0:fact.rb:1:Module:<: def fact(n)
#0:fact.rb:10::-: print fact(ARGV[0].to_i), "\n"
#0:fact.rb:10:Array:>: print fact(ARGV[0].to_i), "\n"
#0:fact.rb:10:Array:<: print fact(ARGV[0].to_i), "\n"
#0:fact.rb:10:String:>: print fact(ARGV[0].to_i), "\n"
#0:fact.rb:10:String:<: print fact(ARGV[0].to_i), "\n"
#0:fact.rb:1:Object:>: def fact(n)
#0:fact.rb:2:Object:-:    return 1 if n == 0
#0:fact.rb:2:Fixnum:>:    return 1 if n == 0
#0:fact.rb:2:Fixnum:<:    return 1 if n == 0
#0:fact.rb:3:Object:-:    f = 1
#0:fact.rb:4:Object:-:    while n>0
#0:fact.rb:4:Fixnum:>:    while n>0
#0:fact.rb:4:Fixnum:<:    while n>0
#0:fact.rb:5:Object:-:      f *= n
#0:fact.rb:5:Fixnum:>:      f *= n
#0:fact.rb:5:Fixnum:<:      f *= n
#0:fact.rb:6:Object:-:      n -= 1
#0:fact.rb:6:Fixnum:>:      n -= 1
#0:fact.rb:6:Fixnum:<:      n -= 1
#0:fact.rb:6:Fixnum:>:      n -= 1
#0:fact.rb:6:Fixnum:<:      n -= 1
#0:fact.rb:5:Object:-:      f *= n
#0:fact.rb:5:Fixnum:>:      f *= n
#0:fact.rb:5:Fixnum:<:      f *= n
#0:fact.rb:6:Object:-:      n -= 1
#0:fact.rb:6:Fixnum:>:      n -= 1
#0:fact.rb:6:Fixnum:<:      n -= 1
#0:fact.rb:6:Fixnum:>:      n -= 1
#0:fact.rb:6:Fixnum:<:      n -= 1
#0:fact.rb:8:Object:-:    return f
#0:fact.rb:8:Object:<:    return f
#0:fact.rb:10:Kernel:>: print fact(ARGV[0].to_i), "\n"
#0:fact.rb:10:IO:>: print fact(ARGV[0].to_i), "\n"
#0:fact.rb:10:Fixnum:>: print fact(ARGV[0].to_i), "\n"
#0:fact.rb:10:Fixnum:<: print fact(ARGV[0].to_i), "\n"
2#0:fact.rb:10:IO:<: print fact(ARGV[0].to_i), "\n"
#0:fact.rb:10:IO:>: print fact(ARGV[0].to_i), "\n"

#0:fact.rb:10:IO:<: print fact(ARGV[0].to_i), "\n"
#0:fact.rb:10:Kernel:<: print fact(ARGV[0].to_i), "\n"
```

You can turn on trace mode explicitly by invoking these methods from your program:

`Tracer.on`
> Turns on trace mode

`Tracer.on {...}`
> Evaluates the block with trace mode turned on

`Tracer.off`
> Turns off trace mode

irb

irb (Interactive Ruby) was developed by Keiju Ishitsuka. It allows you to enter commands at the prompt and have the interpreter respond as if you were executing a program. `irb` is useful to experiment with or to explore Ruby.

> irb [*options*] [*programfile*] [*argument...*]

Here are the `irb` options:

`-f` Suppresses loading of ~/.irbrc.

`-m` Math mode. Performs calculations using rational numbers.

`-d` Debugger mode. Sets $DEBUG to `true`.

`-r` *lib*
> Uses `require` to load the library *lib* before executing the program.

`-v`
`--version`
> Displays the version of `irb`.

`--inspect`
> Inspect mode (default).

`--noinspect`
> Noninspect mode (default for math mode).

`--readline`
> Uses the `readline` library.

`--noreadline`
> Suppresses use of the `readline` library.

`--prompt` *mode*
`--prompt-mode` *mode*
> Sets the prompt mode. Predefined prompt modes are `default`, `simple`, `xmp`, and `inf-ruby`.

`--inf-ruby-mode`
> Sets the prompt mode to `inf-ruby` and suppresses use of the `readline` library.

`--simple-prompt`
> Sets the prompt mode to simple mode.

```
--noprompt
```
Suppresses the prompt display.

```
--tracer
```
Displays a trace of method calls.

```
--back-trace-limit n
```
Sets the depth of backtrace information to be displayed (default is 16).

Here is a sample irb interaction:

```
irb
irb(main):001:0> a = 25
25
irb(main):002:0> a = 2
2
irb(main):003:0>
matz@ev[sample] irb
irb(main):001:0> a = 3
3
irb(main):002:0> a.times do |i|
irb(main):003:1* puts i
irb(main):004:1> end
0
1
2
3
irb(main):005:0> class Foo<Object
irb(main):006:1> def foo
irb(main):007:2> puts "foo"
irb(main):008:2> end
irb(main):009:1> end
nil
irb(main):010:0> Foo::new.foo
foo
nil
irb(main):011:0> exit
```

irb loads a startup file from either ~/.irbrc, .irbrc, irb.rc, _irbrc, $irbrc.
A Startup file can contain an arbitrary Ruby program for per-user configuration.
Within it, irb context object IRB is available.

irb works as if you fed the program line by line into the interpreter. But since the
noninteractive interpreter executes the program at once, there is a small difference. For example, in batch execution, the local variable that appears only in the
eval isn't treated as a local variable outside of eval. That's because an identifier
is determined as a local variable or not statically. In non-irb mode, Ruby determines whether or not an identifier is a local variable during compile-time. Since
Ruby compiles the whole program first and then executes it, assignment in eval
isn't considered. But in irb mode, irb normally executes inputs line by line, so
that assignment is done prior to compilation of the next line.

ruby-mode for Emacs

If you are an Emacs user, ruby-mode will help you a lot. It supports auto indent, colorizing program text, etc. To use ruby-mode, put *ruby-mode.el* into the directory included in your load-path variable, then put the following code in your *.emacs* file.

```
(autoload 'ruby-mode "ruby-mode" "Mode for editing ruby source files" t)
(setq auto-mode-alist (append '(("\\.rb$" .ruby-mode))
        auto-mode-alist))
(setq interpreter-mode-alist (append '(("ruby".ruby-mode))
        interpreter-mode-alist))
```

Additional Tools

There are other useful tools that don't come bundled with the Ruby standard distribution. However, you do need to install them yourself.

ri: Ruby Interactive Reference

ri is a online reference tool developed by Dave Thomas, the famous pragmatic programmer. When you have a question about the behavior of a certain method, e.g., IO#gets, you can invoke ri IO#gets to read the brief explanation of the method. You can get ri from *http://www.pragmaticprogrammer.com/ruby/downloads/ri.html*.

    ri [options] [name...]

Here are the ri options:

--version,
-v

>   Displays version and exits.

--line-length=n
-l n

>   Sets the line length for the output (minimum is 30 characters).

--synopsis
-s

>   Displays just a synopsis.

--format=*name*
-f *name*

>   Uses the *name* module (default is Plain) for output formatting. Here are the available modules:

>   *Tagged*
>>   Simple tagged output

>   *Plain*
>>   Default plain output

name should be specified in any of the following forms:

— `Class`

— `Class::method`

— `Class#method`

— `Class.method`

— `method`

eRuby

eRuby stands for embedded Ruby; it's a tool that embeds fragments of Ruby code in other files such as HTML files. Here's a sample eRuby file:

```
This is sample eRuby file<br>
The current time here is <%=Time.now%>.
<%[1,2,3].each{|x|print x,"<br>\n"}%>
```

Here's the output from this sample file:

```
This is sample eRuby file<br>
The current time here is Wed Aug 29 18:54:45 JST 2001.
1
2
3
```

There are two eRuby implementations:

eruby

The original implementation of eRuby. eruby is available from *http://www.modruby.net.*

Erb

A pure Ruby (subset) implementation of eRuby.

eRuby is available from *http://www2a.biglobe.ne.jp/~seki/ruby/erb-1.3.3.tar.gz*; The version number may be changed in the future. Unfortunately, the supporting page *http://www2a.biglobe.ne.jp/~seki/ruby/* is in Japanese, but you can tell how to use it from its source code.

Ruby Application Archive

Do you want to access databases, such as PostgreSQL or MySQL from Ruby? Do you wish to use such nonstandard GUI toolkits as Qt, Gtk, FOX, etc.? You can with the Ruby Application Archive (RAA), which has a collection of Ruby programs, libraries, documentations, and binary packages compiled for specific platforms. You can access RAA at *http://www.ruby-lang.org/en/raa.html.* RAA is still far smaller than Perl's CPAN, but it's growing every day.

RAA contains the following elements:

• The latest 10 items

• A list of Ruby applications

- A list of Ruby libraries
- A list of Ruby porting
- A list of Ruby documents

You can enter your program in RAA by clicking "add new entry" at the top of the RAA page, then following the instructions there. RAA itself is a fully automated web application written in Ruby. It uses eRuby and PStore as a backend.

CHAPTER 6

Ruby Updates

Compared to most other languages, Ruby is rather young. As a result, it's still evolving fairly rapidly.

If you find a bug in Ruby, the first thing to do is to check the bug database and see if the problem has already been reported. The bug database can be found at *http://www.ruby-lang.org/cgi-bin/ruby-bugs*. You can either send the bug report directly from that page or send an email to *ruby-bugs@ruby-lang.org*. When you submit your bug, try to include all relevant information such as source code, operating system, the output from ruby -v, and what version/build of Ruby you are running. If you have compiled your own build of Ruby, you should also include the rbconfig.rb.

The current stable version of Ruby can always be found at *http://www.ruby-lang.org/en/download.html*. There are also several mirror sites available.

The current developmental release can be obtained from the CVS (Concurrent Version System) repository. See *http://www.ruby-lang.org/en/cvsrepo.html* for instructions. You can get CVS tools from *http://www.cvshome.com*.

Summary of Changes

Developmental releases of Ruby always have an odd minor revision number such as 1.5 or 1.7. Once a developmental release is stable and finalized, it's then "promoted" to a stable release. Stable releases always have an even minor revision number such as 2.0 or 3.2. Therefore, releases with even subversion numbers (1.4, 1.6, 1.8, etc.) are stable releases. Releases with odd subversion numbers (1.5, 1.7, etc.) are developmental versions and are available only from the CVS repository.

At of the writing of this book, the current stable release version is 1.6.5. The current developmental version is 1.7.1. The changes presented here are currently

176

reflected in 1.7.1 and will probably remain relatively unchanged in the next stable release—Version 1.8.

Changes from 1.6.5 to 1.7.1

The following information details the changes that are occurring in development versions 1.7.1 and 1.8 (though 1.8 will have additional changes as well):

- Multiple assignment behavior is clarified.

- Syntax enhanced to interpret argument parentheses to allow p ("xx"*2).to_i.

- break and next extended to take an optional expression, which is used as a return value of the iterating method and yield, respectively.

- The following new methods (or modifications to methods) have been added:

```
Array#fetch
Array#insert
Enumerable#all?
Enumerable#any?
Enumerable#inject
Enumerable#sort_by
File#fnmatch
MatchData#to_ary
Method#==
Module#include?
Module#included
Module#method_removed
Module#method_undefined
Object#singleton_method_removed
Object#singleton_method_undefined
Proc#==
Proc#yield
Range#to_ary
Range#step
Regexp#options
String#casecmp
String#insert
Symbol#intern
Symbol::all_symbols
SystemExit#status
File::lchmod
File::lchown
IO::for_fd
IO::read
Math::acos
Math::asin
Math::atan
Math::cosh
Math::hypot
Math::sinh
```

```
Math::tanh
Process::times
Process::waitall
SystemCallError::===
```

- `String#eql?` is now always case-sensitive.

- `Dir::chdir` extended to take a block.

- `NoMethodError` raised for undefined method.

- `Interrupt` is a subclass of `SignalException` (it was a subclass of Exception in 1.6 and prior).

- `$?` now gives `Process::Status` along with `Process::wait2`, `Process::waitpid2`.

- `Regexp.last_match(n)` extended to take an optional argument.

- The `Digest` module has been added as a replacement for the `md5` and `sha1` modules.

- Line-range operation is now obsolete except when used in a one-liner (e.g., `ruby -e ...`).

- Comparison of exception classes in a rescue clause now uses `Module#===`.

- `TCPSocket.new` and `TCPSocket.open` extended to take an address and a port number for the local side in optional third and fourth arguments.

- `Time` extended to accept a negative `time_t` (only if the platform supports it).

- Objects that have `to_str` now behave more like strings.

- The `Signal` module has been added.

- Generational garbage collection has been added.

The Future of Ruby

As Ruby is now used by so many programmers worldwide, I don't see making any radical changes in the near future. But I'd like to keep Ruby competitive with other scripting languages.

I don't have a concrete plan for future versions, even 2.0, but I do have plans to fix some of the remaining drawbacks in the Ruby implementation. For example, Ruby's internals are too complex to maintain and can be slower than other languages. I'm going to reimplement the interpreter as a bytecode engine to simplify interpreter core and boost performance. Also, recently an intriguing but still vague possibility of a joint backend among Perl, Python, and Ruby has surfaced.

I'd also like to support M17N (Multilingualization) in Ruby. M17N offers the ability to handle various human languages along with the necessary encodings. We already implemented a prototype that can handle ASCII, UTF-8, and several Japanese encodings.

The future is unknown, and my imagination is limited. But you can certainly contribute to the evolution of Ruby via the process called RCR (or Ruby Change Requests) explained in the next section. We look forward to your contributions.

Participate in Ruby

Programmers often get ideas on how they'd like to improve Ruby. These ideas are sometimes useful and interesting, sometimes not. Since the language needs to stay consistent, I often need to choose which fixes or ideas to add and which to reject. To make this process easier, we have instituted Ruby Change Requests (RCRs).

When you want to propose a new feature for Ruby, you have to submit your proposal to *http://www.rubygarden.org/?topic=RCR*. The more concrete and detailed the proposal, the greater chance of success you have of getting it accepted. The proposal should preferably be consistent, backward-compatible, and follow the principle of least surprise.

The RCR page offers a discussion forum and web-based voting box. Once you submit your proposal, discussion is held on it. If it's decided (with the help of the community) that your proposal is indeed useful, it will be added to future versions of Ruby.

Index

Symbols

<=>
  Comparable module, 73
  Date instance method, 162
  File::Stat instance method, 83
  Module instance method, 96
  Time instance method, 107

& (ampersand)
  Array instance method, 59
  FalseClass instance method, 103
  HTML special character, 130
  Integer instance method, 71
  logical operators, 19
  TrueClass instance method, 103

* (asterisk)
  $* variable, 38
  Array instance method, 59
  as control character, 13
  directives and, 63
  Matrix instance method, 156
  Numeric instance method, 69
  parallel assignments and, 17
  Rational class and, 154
  String class methods and, 50

@ (at sign)
  instance variables and, 15
  $@ variable, 36

\ (backslash)
  at end of line, 8
  control characters and, 13
  predefined variable, 36
  strings and, 10
  while statement and, 26

{} (braces)
  as control character, 13
  as string delimiter, 11
  local variables and, 15

[] (brackets)
  array expressions and, 12
  as control characters, 13

^ (caret)
  as control character, 13
  FalseClass instance method, 104
  Integer instance method, 71
  TrueClass instance method, 103

: (colon)
  separating paths with, 7

, (comma), 36

$ (dollar sign)
  as control character, 13
  global variables and, 15
  predefined variable, 37

= (equal sign)
  abbreviated assignments and, 17
  accessor methods and, 32
  case statement and, 26
  Comparable instance method, 74
  Module instance method, 96

We'd like to hear your suggestions for improving our indexes. Send email to *index@oreilly.com*.

Range instance method, 104
Regexp instance method, 57
String class methods and, 50
! (exclamation point)
  appending to methods, 20
  Array class methods, 59
  Hash class and, 65
  String class methods and, 50
  string delimiter, 11
> (greater than sign)
  Comparable instance method, 74
  HTML special character, 130
  Module instance method, 96
  predefined variable, 36
  Time instance method, 107
>> (greater than signs)
  Date instance method, 162
  Integer instance method, 71
< (less than sign)
  as string delimiter, 11
  Comparable instance method, 74
  HTML special character, 130
  Module instance method, 96
  Time instance method, 107
<< (less than sign)
  abbreviated assignments and, 17
<< (less than signs)
  Array instance method, 60
  Curses::Window class and, 138
  Date instance method, 162
  Integer instance method, 71
  IO instance method, 76
  MD5 instance method, 165
  SHA1 instance method, 165
  String class methods and, 50
- (minus sign)
  Array instance method, 59
  at end of line, 8
  Date instance method, 162
  Matrix instance method, 156
  Numeric instance method, 69
  Time instance method, 107
() (parentheses)
  as control characters, 13
  as string delimiter, 11
% (percent)
  as conversion specifier, 44
  directives and, 108
  Numeric instance method, 69
  String class methods and, 50
  wildcard patterns, 123

. (period)
  as control character, 13
  IO instance method, 76
  predefined variable, 36
+ (plus sign)
  Array instance method, 59
  as control character, 13
  at end of line, 8
  Date instance method, 162
  Matrix instance method, 156
  Numeric instance method, 69
  predefined variable, 38
  String class methods and, 50
  Time instance method, 107
(pound sign)
  comment and, 14
  comments and, 8
  expression substitution, 10
? (question mark)
  appending to methods, 20
  as control character, 13
  predefined variable, 37
  ternary operator, 19
  test() function and, 45
" (quotation marks)
  as empty strings, 146
  delimited strings and, 11
  predefined variables, 38
  strings and, 10
; (semicolon)
  begin statement and, 28
  case statement and, 26
  for statement and, 27
  if statement and, 25
  interpretation of, 8
  separating paths with, 7
  until statement and, 26
  while statement and, 26
~ (tilde)
  expanding, 7
  Integer instance method, 71
  local variable, 37
  Regexp instance method, 57
  String class methods and, 50
_ (underscore), 9, 15
  $_ variable, 37, 40, 41, 42, 45
| (vertical bar)
  abbreviated assignments and, 17
  Array instance method, 59
  as control character, 13
  FalseClass instance method, 103

Integer instance method, 71
open() function and, 42
TrueClass instance method, 103
/ (slash)
  Matrix instance method, 156
  Numeric instance method, 69
  predefined variable, 36
  regular expressions and, 12

A

-a option, 5, 37
abort
  Kernel, 39
  Net::FTP, 118
  PStore, 153
  security level 4 and, 35
abort_on_exception (Thread), 91, 92
abs
  Complex, 154
  Numeric, 69
abs2 (Complex), 154
accept
  Socket, 117
  UNIXServer, 116
accessors
  CGI class, 134
  CGI::Cookie class, 134
  methods, 32
acct (Net::FTP), 118
add
  IPSocket, 112
  ThreadGroup, 93
add_authenticator (Net::IMAP), 122
addch (Curses), 136, 138
add_observer (Observable), 160
addr
  Socket, 117
  UNIXSocket, 115
addstr (Curses), 137, 138
alias statement, 23
alias_method (Module), 97
alive? (Thread), 92
all (Net::POPMail), 126
all_waits (ThreadsWait), 151
ancestors (Module), 96
append (Net::IMAP), 122
append_features (Module), 97
arc tangent, atan2() and, 74
arg (Complex), 154
ARGF constant, 36, 37, 38
ArgumentError class, 94

arguments
  accessor methods and, 32
  calls method and, 20
  def statement, 22
  GetoptLong class and, 143, 145
  interpreting, 6
  new method and, 32
ARGV constant, 33, 38
arity
  Method, 101
  Proc, 100
Array class, 59–64
Array function, 39
arrays
  as container classes, 12
  def statement arguments and, 22
  delimited string, 12
  select() function and, 43
  to_a and, 49, 59
  unpack(), 55
  (see also specific methods for Array
     class)
ASCII
  Ruby support for, 178
  specifying, 6
asctime (Time), 107
assignments, 16–17
assoc (Array), 60
at
  Array, 60
  Time, 106
atan2 (Math), 74
at_exit (Kernel), 39
atime (File), 79, 82, 83
attr, 97
attr (Module), 97
attr_accessor (Module), 97
attributes
  as variables, 32
  assignments and, 17
  CGI class, 134
  Struct class and, 105
  tags common to HTML, 133
attr_reader (Module), 97
attr_writer (Module), 98
authentication
  Net::APOP class and, 125
  Net::IMAP class and, 122
authenticate (Net::IMAP), 122
autoload (Kernel), 35, 39

B

b (conversion specifier), 44
backslash notation, 10, 52
backspace, 14
backtrace (Exception), 93
--back-trace-limit option (irb), 172
basename (File), 79
BasicSocket class, 111, 112, 115
beep (Curses), 137
=begin, embedded documents and, 8
begin
    MatchData, 58
    Range, 104
begin statement, 28, 29
begx (Curses::Window), 138
begy (Curses::Window), 138
between? (Comparable), 74
Bignum class, 9, 72
binary integers, conversion specifiers
        and, 44
bind
    Socket, 117
    UDPSocket, 113
    UnboundMethod, 101
binding function, 39, 101
binmode (Net::Telnet), 128
blksize (File::Stat), 83
blockdev? (File), 79, 83, 86
block_given? (Kernel), 39
blocks
    begin statement and, 28
    block_given? function and, 39
    each_line() and, 52
    initializing, 32
    variable scope in, 21
blocks (File::Stat), 84
box (Curses::Window), 139
break statement, 27
broadcast (ConditionVariable), 148

C

-C option, 5
-c option, 5
c (conversion specifier), 44
calendars, Julian and Gregorian, 161
call
    Continuation, 102
    Method, 101
    Proc, 100
    redo statement and, 27
    Win32API, 147
callcc (Kernel), 39
caller (Kernel), 39
capability (Net::IMAP), 122
capitalize (String), 51
capitalize! (String), 51
case statements, 26, 57
casefold? (Regexp), 57
catch (Kernel), 39, 46
cbreak (Curses), 137
ceil (Numeric), 69
center (String), 51
CGI class, 129–132, 134
CGI (Common Gateway Interface), 34,
        129
CGI::Cookie class, 131, 134
CGI::Session class, 135, 136
changed (Observable), 160
changed? (Observable), 160
characters
    control, 13
    conversion specifiers and, 44
    deleting, 137
    deleting from string, 51, 52
    HTML special, 130
    outputting to screen, 136
    reading screen, 137
    replacing in string, 55
    reversing in string, 53
    upper and lowercase, 9
chardev?
    File, 79
    File::Stat, 84
    FileTest, 86
chdir
    Dir, 34, 87
    Net::FTP, 118
check (Net::IMAP), 122
checkbox (CGI), 131
checkbox_group (CGI), 131
checksum, sum() and, 55
chmod (File), 34, 79, 142
chmode (File), 82
chomp
    Kernel, 40
    String, 51
chomp!
    Kernel, 40
    String, 51
chop
    Kernel, 40
    String, 51

chop!,
  Kernel, 40
  String, 51
chown (File), 34, 79, 82
chr (Integer), 71
chroot (Dir), 34, 87
Class class, 29, 30, 99
class (Kernel), 48
class statement, 21, 30
class variables, 15
class_eval (Class), 99
class_variables (Module), 96
clear
  Array, 60
  Curses, 137
  Curses::Window, 139
  Hash, 65
clone
  Kernel, 48
  MD5, 164
  SHA1, 165
close
  Curses::Window, 139
  database manager, 136
  DBM, 152
  Dir, 88
  IO, 76
  Net::FTP, 118
  Net::IMAP, 122
  Tempfile, 147
closed?
  IO, 76
  Net::FTP, 118
close_read (IO), 76
close_screen (Curses), 137
close_write (IO), 76
cmd (Net::Telnet), 128
cmp (File), 142
coerce (Numeric), 69
collect! (Array), 60
collect
  Array, 60
  Enumerable, 67
  Matrix, 156
cols (Curses), 137
column (Matrix), 156
columns (Matrix), 155
column_size (Matrix), 156
column_vector (Matrix), 155
column_vectors (Matrix), 156
command-line options, 5–6, 143, 166

commands
  cmd() and, 128
  debugger, 166–168
  exec() function and, 40
  File::open() and, 80
  NOOP command, 123
  open() function and, 42
  system() function and, 45
  trap() function and, 46
  untrace_var() function and, 46
comments, 8, 14
commit (PStore), 153
compact (Array), 60
compact! (Array), 60
Comparable module
  built-in library, 73
  File::Stat object and, 83
  included in Date class, 161
  Numeric class and, 69
  String class and, 50
  Time class and, 106
compare (File), 142
compile (Regexp), 57
completion_append_character
      (Readline), 146
completion_case_fold (Readline), 146
completion_proc (Readline), 146
Complex class, 154
COMSPEC, spawned processes and, 8
concat
  Array, 60
  String, 51
concatenation, 10, 50
conditional statements, 18, 25–27
ConditionVariable class, 148
conjugate (Complex), 154
connect
  Net::FTP instance method, 118
  Socket instance method, 117
  UDPSocket instance method, 113
constants
  assignments and, 16
  built-in library, 75
  classes and, 30
  Date class, 163
  Fcntl module and, 141
  File class, 82
  GetoptLong class, 144
  identifiers as, 9
  predefined global, 38
  Process module and, 90

constants (*continued*)
  pseudo-variables and, 16
  Readline module, 146
  Socket class, 117
  ThreadGroup class and, 93
  uppercase letter, 16
constants (Module), 96
const_defined? (Module), 96
const_get (Module), 96
const_set (Module), 96
Continuation class, 102
control structures, 25–29
conversion specifiers, 44
cookies (CGI), 131
copy
  File, 142
  Net::IMAP, 122
--copyright option, 6
cos (Math), 74
count (String), 51
count_observers (Observable), 160
cp (File), 142
create (Net::IMAP), 122
critical (Thread), 91
crmode (Curses), 137
crypt (String), 51
ctime
  File, 79, 82
  File::Stat, 84
  Time, 107
current (Thread), 91
Curses module, 136
Curses::Window class, 138–139
cursors, manipulating, 138
curx (Curses::Window), 139
cury (Curses::Window), 139
CVS (Concurrent Version System)
      web site, 176
cwday (Date), 162
cweek (Date), 162
cwyear (Date), 162

D

-d option, 5, 37, 171
d (conversion specifier), 44
DATA constant, 38
data persistence, 151
data retrieval, 140
data wrapper, 104
database manager, 136

databases, 152, 174
Date class, 161–163
date formatting, 130
day
  Date, 162
  Time, 107
DAYNAMES constant, 163
DBM class, 152
$DEBUG (predefined variable), 5, 37, 171
debug mode
  enabling parser, 6
  returning status, 118
  setting, 5
debug (Net::IMAP), 122
--debug option, 6, 37
debugger, 166–169
debugging
  p() function and, 42
  Ruby bug database, 176
  set_trace_func() function, 43
debug_mode (Net::FTP), 118
decimals, 44, 63
def statement
  agruments for, 22
  class methods and, 30
  local variables and, 21
  singleton methods and, 22
Default (constant), 93
default (Hash), 65
def_delegator
  Forwardable, 159
  SingleForwardable, 159
def_delegators
  Forwardable, 159
  SingleForwardable, 159
defined?
  operator, 19
define_finalizer (ObjectSpace), 102
def_instance_delegator
    (Forwardable), 159
def_instance_delegators
    (Forwardable), 159
$defout
  predefined variable, 36, 37
  printf() function and, 42
  putc() function and, 42
  puts() function and, 43
def_singleton_delegator
    (SingleForwardable), 159
def_singleton_delegators
    (SingleForwardable), 159

delch
  Curses, 137
  Curses::Window, 139
DelegateClass (DelegatorClass), 158
Delegator class, 158
DelegatorClass class, 158
delete
  Array, 60
  CGI::Session, 136
  database manager, 136
  Dir, 88
  File, 79
  Hash, 65
  Net::FTP, 119
  Net::IMAP, 122
  Net::POPMail, 126
  String c, 52
delete! (String), 52
delete_at (Array), 60
deleted? (Net::POPMail), 126
delete_if
  Array, 60
  Hash, 65
deleteln
  Curses, 137
  Curses::Window, 139
delete_observer (Observable), 160
delete_observers (Observable), 160
delimiters, 11, 12
design patterns, 158, 159
det (Matrix), 156
detect (Enumerable), 67
determinant (Matrix), 156
dev (File::Stat), 84
diagonal (Matrix), 155
digest
  MD5, 164
  SHA1, 165
Dir class, 34, 87–88
dir (Net::FTP), 119
directives
  decimals and, 63
  packing array elements, 62
  t.strftime() and, 108
directories
  changing, 5, 118
  creating, 119, 142
  data retrieval with Etc module, 140
  loading libraries, 5

  removing, 120
  security level 1 and, 34
  traversal of, 141
directory?
  File, 79
  File::Stat, 84
  FileTest, 86
dirname (File), 79
disable (GC), 102
disconnect (Net::IMAP), 123
display (Kernel), 48
divmod (Numeric), 70
DLN_LIBRARY_PATH (environment
        variable), 7
do (reserved word), 27
do_not_reverse_lookup
        (BasicSocket), 111
doupdate (Curses), 137
downcase (String), 52
downto
  Date, 162
  Integer, 71
dump
  Marshal, 104
  String, 52
dup (Kernel), 48
dynamic programming, 2

E
-e option, 5, 34
E (constant), 75
E (conversion specifier), 44
e (conversion specifier), 44
each
  Array, 60
  Dir, 88
  Enumerable, 67
  GetoptLong, 144
  Hash, 65
  IO, 76
  method example, 2
  Net::POP3, 125
  Range, 104
  String, 52
  Struct, 106
each_byte
  IO, 76
  String, 52
each_index (Array), 61

each_key (Hash), 65
each_line
  IO, 76
  String, 52
each_object (ObjectSpace), 103
each_option (GetoptLong), 144
each_pair (Hash), 65
each_value (Hash), 65
each_with_index (Enumerable), 67
echo (Curses), 137
editors, 146
egid (Process), 32, 34, 89
else clause, 22, 26, 28
Emacs editor, 146, 173
emacs_editing_mode (Readline), 146
empty?
  Array, 61
  Hash, 65
  Queue, 150
  String, 52
  ThreadsWait, 151
enable (GC method), 102
=end, embedded documents and, 8
end (MatchData), 58
end (Range), 105
end statement, 29, 39
ENGLAND constant, 163
enq (Queue), 150
ensure clause, 22, 26, 28
enter (Monitor), 148
entries
  Dir, 87
  Enumerable, 68
Enumerable module
  Array class and, 59
  built-in library, 67–69
  Dir class and, 87
  Hash class, 64
  included for DBM class, 152
  IO class and, 75
  String class and, 50
Enumerated module, 104
ENV constant, 38
ENV object, 7
environment variables, 7, 33, 35
eof (IO), 76
eof? (IO), 76
EOFError, 43, 94
eql? (Kernel), 48
equal? (Kernel), 48
Erb, eRuby implementation, 174

Errno::ENOENT class, 94, 95
Errno::EPERM class, 95
error (GetoptLong), 144
error? (GetoptLong), 144
error_message (GetoptLong), 144
eRuby (embedded Ruby), 174
eruby, original eRuby
      implementation, 174
escape
  CGI, 130
  Regexp, 57
escapeElement (CGI), 130
escapeHTML (CGI), 130
Etc module, 140
EUC (Extended Unix Code), 6
euid (Process), 89
eval, 34, 40
examine (Net::IMAP), 123
Exception class, 93–95
exception (Exception), 93
exception handling, 3, 28, 29, 93
exec() function, 40
executable?
  File, 79
  File::Stat, 84
  FileTest, 86
executable_real?
  File, 79
  File::Stat, 84
  FileTest, 86
exist?
  Date, 161
  File, 79
  FileTest, 86
exist2? (Date), 161
exist3? (Date), 161
existw? (Date), 161
exit
  Kernel, 40
  Monitor, 148
  security level 4 and, 35
  Thread, 91, 92
exit!
  Kernel, 40
  Process, 89
  security level 2 and, 34
exp (Math), 74
expand_path (File), 79
exponential function, 74
exponential notation, 44
expressions, 10, 12

expunge (Net::IMAP), 123
ext, as file extension, 5
extend
    adding properties with, 31
    Kernel, 48
extend_object (Module), 98
extensions, 5, 43

F

$F (predefined variable), 37
-F option, 5
-f option, 171
f (conversion specifier), 44
factorial function, 2
fail function, 40, 43
FALSE constant, 38
false (pseudo-variable), 16
FalseClass class, 103
Fatal class, 95
fcntl (IO), 76
Fcntl module, 141
fetch
    Hash, 65
    Net::IMAP, 123
_ _FILE_ _
    pseudo-variable, 16
File class, 34, 78, 142, 147
file?
    File, 79
    File::Stat, 84
    FileTest, 86
File::Constants module, 82
file_field (CGI), 131
$FILENAME (predefined variable), 37
fileno (IO), 76
files
    comparing, 142
    copying, 142, 143
    deleting, 119
    moving, 143
    removing, 143
    renaming, 120
    retrieving remote, 119
    test() function and, 45
    transferring, 119
    (see also Tempfile class)
File::Separator, 80
File::Stat object, 83–85
FileTest module, 34, 85
fill (Array), 61

find
    Enumerable, 68
    Find, 142
Find module, 142
find_all (Enumerable), 68
finish
    Net::HTTP, 121
    Net::POP3, 125
    Net::SMTP, 127
finished? (ThreadsWait), 151
finite? (Float), 73
first
    Array, 61
    Range, 104
Fixnum class, 9, 23, 29, 72
flags, conversion specifiers and, 44
flash (Curses), 137
flatten (Array), 61
flatten! (Array), 61
Float class, 9, 73
Float, 41, 55
FloatDomainError class, 94
floating point numbers
    conversion specifiers and, 44
    converting from integers, 72
    converting from string, 55
    Float() function and, 41
    rand() function and, 43
    support for, 9
flock (File), 82
floor (Numeric), 70
flush (IO), 76
-fname option, 173
for statement, 27
foreach
    Dir, 87
    IO, 75
for_fd (Socket), 116
fork
    Kernel, 41
    Process, 89
    security level 2 and, 34
    Thread, 91
form (CGI), 131
format function, 41, 44
--format option, 173
formatting date and time, 130
Forwardable module, 159
fractions, 74
freeze (Kernel), 48
frexp (Math), 74

frozen? (Kernel), 48
ftools library, 142
FTP (File Transfer Protocol), 118, 120
ftype
  File, 80
  File::Stat, 84
functions
  built-in, 39–46
  factorial, 2
  methods as, 20
  timeout procedure, 164

G

G (conversion specifier), 44
g (conversion specifier), 44
garbage collection, 3, 102, 146
garbage_collect
  (GC), 102
  (ObjectSpace), 103
GC module, 102
GDBM class, 152
get
  GetoptLong, 144
  Net::HTTP, 121
getaddress (IPSocket), 112
getaddrinfo (Socket), 116
getbinaryfile (Net::FTP), 119
getc (IO), 77
getch
  Curses, 137
  Curses::Window, 139
getdir (Net::FTP), 119
getgrgid (Etc), 140
getgrnam (Etc), 140
gethostbyaddr (Socket), 116
gethostbyname (Socket), 116
gethostname (Socket), 116
getlogin (Etc), 140
getnameinfo (Socket), 117
__getobj__ (Delegator), 157
get_option (GetoptLong), 144
GetoptLong class, 143–144
getpeername (BasicSocket), 111
getpgid (Process), 89
getpgrp (Process), 89
getpriority (Process), 89
getpty (PTY), 145
getpwnam (Etc), 140
getpwuid (Etc), 140
gets, 37, 41, 77
getservbyname (Socket), 117

getsockname (BasicSocket), 111
getsockopt (BasicSocket), 111
getstr
  Curses, 137
  Curses::Window, 139
gettextfile (Net::FTP), 119
getwd (Dir), 88
gid
  File::Stat, 84
  Process, 89
glob (Dir), 87
global variables, 15, 16, 46
global_variables (Kernel), 41
gm (Time), 106
gmt? (Time), 109
gmtime (Time), 107
gmtime? (Time), 107
GNU line editing library, 145, 152
greeting (Net::IMAP), 123
Gregorian calendar, 161
GREGORIAN constant, 163
grep (Enumerable), 68
group (Etc), 141
grpowned?
  File, 80
  File::Stat, 84
  FileTest, 86
gsub, 41, 52
gsub!, 41, 52

H

-h option, 5
Hash class, 64–67, 152
hashes
  CGI::Session class and, 135
  databases and, 152
  ENV as, 38
  eq?() method and, 48
  key-value pairs, 12
  method calls and, 20
has_key?
  CGI, 131
  Hash, 66
has_value? (Hash), 67
head (Net::HTTP), 121
header
  CGI, 131
  Net::POPMail, 126
help (Net::FTP), 119
--help option, 6
help options, 5, 6, 119

here documents, 11
hex (String), 52
hexadecimals, 44, 52
hexdigest
  MD5, 165
  SHA1, 165
hidden (CGI), 131
HIDDEN field, 131
HISTORY constant, 146
HOME (environment variable), 7
hooks, 32
hour (Time), 107
HTML (Hyper Text Markup Language)
  CGI class and, 129
  eRuby and, 174
  generation methods, 132
  new() and, 130
html3 tags, 133
html4 tags, 133
html4Fr tags, 133
html4Tr tags, 133
htmlFr tags, 133
HTTP (Hyper Text Transfer Protocol)
  CGI class and, 129
  CGI::Cookie class, 134
  CGI::Session class and, 135
  Net::HTTP class and, 120

I

-I option, 5, 34
-i option, 5, 14, 34
i (conversion specifier), 44
I (Matrix), 155
id (Kernel), 48
_id2ref (ObjectSpace), 102
identifiers, 9, 12
identity (Matrix), 155
if (reserved word), 25
if statement, 18, 25
image (Complex), 154
image_button (CGI), 131
IMAP4 (Internet Message Access Protocol
      Version 4), 121
inch
  Curses, 137
  Curses::Window, 139
include
  adding properties with, 31
  Module, 98
  security level 4 and, 35

include?
  Array, 61
  CGI, 131
  Enumerable, 68
  Hash, 66
  String, 52
included_modules (Module), 96
index
  Array, 61
  Hash, 66
  String, 52
IndexError class, 94
indexes
  Array, 61
  Hash, 66
indices
  Array, 61
  Hash, 66
induced_from
  Float, 73
  Integer, 71
infinite? (Float), 73
--inf-ruby-mode option, 171
inherited (Class), 99
initialize (database manager), 136
initialize
  Object class and, 47
  objects and, 32
init_screen (Curses), 137
ino (File::Stat), 84
insch
  Curses, 137
  Curses::Window, 139
inspect
  Kernel, 48
  p() function and, 42
--inspect option, 171
install (File), 142
instance (Singleton), 160
instance variables, 15, 35
instance_eval (Kernel), 48
instance_method (Module), 96
instance_methods (Module), 97
instance_of? (Kernel), 48
instance_variables (Kernel), 48
Integer class, 70–72, 154
Integer, 42, 55
integer? (Numeric), 70
integers
  ceil and, 69
  conversion specifiers and, 44

integers (*continued*)
  converting from string, 55
  floor and, 70
  Integer() function and, 42
  round and, 70
  support for, 9
  trap() function and, 46
interfaces
  Curses module and, 136
  DBM class and, 152
  Readline module and, 145
  SDBM class and, 152
  String#pack and, 116
intern (String), 52
interpreter, 5, 7
interpretive programming, 2
Interrupt class, 95
inv (Matrix), 156
inverse (Matrix), 156
invert (Hash), 66
IO class, 33, 43, 75–78, 111
ioctl (IO), 77
IOError class, 94
IP addresses, 112
IPSocket class, 113, 114
IPv6, 112
irb (Interactive Ruby), 171
is_a? (Kernel), 49
isatty (IO), 77
isdst (Time), 107
Ishitsuka, Keiju, 171
ITALY constant, 163
iterators, 2

J
jd (Date), 162
join
  Array, 61
  File, 80
  Thread, 92
  ThreadsWait, 151
join_nowait (ThreadsWait), 151
Julian calendar, 161, 162
JULIAN constant, 163

K
-K option, 6
Kernel module, 39, 47–50

key?
  CGI, 131
  Hash, 66
  Thread, 92
keys
  CGI, 131
  Hash, 66
  h.default and, 65
kill
  Process, 90
  security level 2 and, 34
  Thread, 91, 92
kind_of? (Kernel), 49

L
-l option, 6
lambda function, 42
last
  Array, 61
  Range, 105
lastresp (Net::FTP), 119
ldexp (Math), 74
leap? (Date), 162
length
  Array, 61
  Hash, 66
  MatchData, 58
  Queue, 150
  Range, 105
  String, 54
lexical conventions, 8
libraries
  built-in, 47
  bundled, 3
  loading, 6
  miscellaneous, 160
  predefined variables in, 36
  require() function and, 43
  search path for, 7
  web site, 3
  _ _LINE_ _ pseudo-variable, 16
--line-length option, 173
lineno (IO), 77
lines (Curses), 137
link (File), 80
list
  Net::FTP, 119
  Net::IMAP, 123

Thread, 91
ThreadGroup, 93
listen (Socket), 117
literals, 9–14
ljust (String), 53
-ln option, 173
load
   Kernel, 42
   Marshal, 104
   security level 1, 34
   security level 2, 35
LoadError class, 95
$LOAD_PATH, 34, 37
local (Time), 106
local variables
   assignments and, 16
   class statements and, 30
   for loop and, 27
   method calls and, 20
   module statements and, 31
   predefined, 37
   pseudo-variables and, 16
   scope in blocks, 21
LocalJumpError class, 94
localtime (Time), 107
local_variables function, 42
lock (Mutex), 149
locked? (Mutex), 149
LOCK_EX constant, 82
LOCK_NB constant, 82
LOCK_SH constant, 82
LOCK_UN constant, 82
log (Math), 74
log10 (Math), 74
LOGDIR (environment variable), 7
logical operators, 19
login
   Net::FTP, 119
   Net::IMAP, 123
   Net::Telnet, 128
logout (Net::IMAP), 123
loop function, 42
loops
   abstraction example, 2
   break statement and, 27
   callcc function and, 39
   placing code within, 6
lowercase characters
   capitalize and, 51
   downcase and, 52
   identifiers as, 9
   local variables and, 15
   swapcase and, 55
   upcase and, 57
ls (Net::FTP), 119
lstat (File), 80, 82
lsub (Net::IMAP), 123

M

-m option, 13, 14, 171
M17N (Multilingualization), 178
mail (Net::POPMail), 126
mailboxes, 122, 123
mails (Net::POP3), 125
main (Thread), 91
makedirs (File), 142
map! (Array), 60
map
   Array, 61
   Enumerable, 68
   Matrix, 156
Marshal module, 104, 153
Mastering Regular Expressions
   (O'Reilly), 12
match (Regexp), 58
MatchData class, 38, 58
Math module, 74, 153
Matrix class, 155, 156
max
   Enumerable, 68
   SizedQueue, 151
maxx (Curses::Window), 139
maxy (Curses::Window), 139
MD5 class, 164
md5 (MD5), 164
mday
   Date, 162
   Time, 107
member?
   Array, 61
   Enumerable, 68
   Hash, 66
members (Struct), 105, 106
message (Exception), 93
messages, 123, 126
method calls, 19, 20
Method class, 49, 101
method groups, 20
method (Kernel), 49
method_added (Module), 98
method_defined? (Module), 97

methods
  accessor methods, 32
  def statement and, 30
  identifiers as, 9
  Kernel instance method, 49
  Ruby, 20–25
  types of visibility, 31
  uninitialized variables and, 15
  version 1.7.1, 177
min
  Enumerable, 68
  Time, 108
minor (Matrix), 156
mjd (Date), 162
mkdir
  Dir, 34, 88
  Net::FTP, 119
mkpath (File), 142
mktime (Time), 106
mode (File::Stat), 84
Module class, 30, 95, 99
module statement, 21, 31
module_eval (Module), 97
module_function (Module), 98
modules
  dynamically loaded, 7
  method groups within, 20
  module statement and, 30
modulo (Numeric), 70
modulus, 70
mo_enter (MonitorMixin), 149
mo_exit (MonitorMixin), 149
mon
  Date, 162
  Time, 108
Monitor class, 148
MonitorMixin module, 148, 149
month
  Date, 162
  Time, 108
MONTHNAMES constant, 163
mon_owner (MonitorMixin), 149
mon_synchronize (MonitorMixin), 149
move
  Curses::Window, 139
  File, 143
mtime
  File, 80, 82
  File::Stat, 85
  Net::FTP, 119

multipart_form (CGI), 131
Mutex class, 149
mv (File), 143

N
-n option, 6, 37
\n option, 14, 138
name
  Class, 99
  Module, 97
NameError, 16, 95
nan? (Float), 73
ndbm library, 152
nesting (Module), 96
Net::APOP class, 126
Net::FTP class, 118–120
Net::HTTP class, 120
Net::IMAP class, 122–125
Net::POP3 class, 125, 126
Net::POPMail class, 126
Net::SMTP class, 127
Net::Telnet class, 127
new
  Array, 59
  CGI, 130
  CGI::Session, 135
  Class, 100
  Complex, 154
  ConditionVariable, 148
  Curses::Window, 138
  Date, 161
  DBM, 152
  Delegator, 157
  DelegatorClass, 158
  Dir, 88
  File, 80
  GetoptLong, 143
  Hash, 65
  initialize method and, 47
  IO, 75
  MD5, 164
  Module, 96
  Net::FTP, 118
  Net::HTTP, 121
  Net::IMAP, 122
  Net::SMTP, 127
  objects and, 32
  Proc, 100
  Queue, 150
  Range, 104

Rational, 155
Regexp, 57
SHA1, 165
SimpleDelegator, 158
SizedQueue, 150
Socket, 117
String, 50
Struct, 105
TCPServer, 114
TCPSocket, 114
Thread, 91
ThreadGroup, 93
ThreadsWait, 151
Time, 106
UDPSocket, 113
UNIXServer, 116
UNIXSocket, 115
Win32API, 147
new1 (Date), 161
new2 (Date), 161
new3 (Date), 161
newline
    begin statement and, 28
    case statement and, 26
    chomp() function and, 40
    for statement and, 27
    if statement and, 25
    input record separator, 36
    interpretation of, 8
    puts() function and, 43
    return key and, 138
    until statement and, 26
    while statement and, 26
    \Z option and, 14
newsg (Date), 162
neww (Date), 161
next
    Date, 162
    Integer, 71
    String, 53
next statement, 27
next! (String), 53
next_wait (ThreadsWait), 151
nil
    error_message and, 144
    float() and, 41
    global constant, 38
    global variables and, 15
    integer() and, 42
    next statement and, 27

pseudo-variable, 16
    select() and, 43
nil? (Kernel), 49
NilClass class, 103
nitems (Array), 61
nl (Curses), 138
nlink (File::Stat), 85
nlst (Net::FTP), 119
nocbreak (Curses), 137
nocrmode (Curses), 137
noecho (Curses), 137
--noinspect option, 171
NoMemoryError class, 94
nonl (Curses), 138
nonzero? (Numeric), 70
noop (Net::IMAP), 123
-noprompt option, 172
noraw (Curses), 138
--noreadline option, 171
notify_observers (Observable), 160
NotImplementedError, 95
now (Time), 106
numbers, 9, 69–75, 153
Numeric class
    as inherited class, 154, 155
    built-in library, 69
    Float objects and, 73
    Integer class and, 71
num_waiting (Queue), 150

O
o (conversion specifier), 44
Object class
    as inherited class, 99, 143
    def statement and, 30
    Kernel module and, 39
    OOP tools and, 47
    security level 4 and, 35
object-oriented programming, 1, 29–33
objects
    initializing, 32
    methods and, 20
    singleton methods and, 22
Objects (built-in library), 47
ObjectSpace module, 102
Observable module, 160
oct (String), 53
octals, 14, 44, 53
off (tracer), 171
offset (MatchData), 58

on (tracer), 171
OOP, 1, 29–33
open
  DBM, 152
  Dir, 88
  File, 80
  Kernel, 42
  Net::FTP, 118
  Socket, 117
  TCPServer, 114
  TCPSocket, 114
  Tempfile, 147
  UDPSocket, 113
  UNIXServer, 116
  UNIXSocket, 115
operating system services, 75–90, 136
operators, 8, 17–20, 22
ordering (GetoptLong), 144
out (CGI), 131
output
  overwriting, 5
  split, 5
owned?
  File, 80
  File::Stat, 85
  FileTest, 86
owner (Monitor), 148

P

-p option, 6, 37
p (Kernel), 42
pack (Array), 62
pair (Socket), 117
params (CGI), 132
parse (CGI), 130
ParseDate module, 163
parsedate (ParseDate), 163
pass (Thread), 91
passive (Net::FTP), 119
passwd (Etc), 141
password_field (CGI), 132
passwords, 140
PATH (environment variable), 6, 7, 33
path
  File, 82
  Tempfile, 147
  UNIXSocket, 115
patterns
  regular-expression, 13
  source and, 58

specifying separator, 5
  wildcards, 87, 123
peeraddr
  IPSocket, 112
  Socket, 117
  UNIXSocket, 115
pid
  IO, 77
  Process, 89
pipe (IO), 75
pipe?
  File, 80
  File::Stat, 85
polar (Complex), 154
pop
  Array, 63
  Net::POPMail, 126
  Queue, 150
POP3 (Post Office Protocol Version
    3), 125
popen (IO), 75
popup_menu (CGI), 132
portability, 3
pos
  Dir, 88
  IO, 77
post (Net::HTTP), 121
post_match (MatchData), 58
ppid (Process), 89
prec (Precision), 73
prec_f (Precision), 73
prec_i (Precision), 73
precision (flag), 44
Precision module, 71, 73
pre_match (MatchData), 58
pretty (CGI), 130
print
  IO, 77
  Kernel, 42
  Net::Telnet, 128
printf
  $defout and, 37
  IO, 77
PRIO_PGRP (constant), 90
PRIO_PROCESS (constant), 90
PRIO_USER (constant), 90
private
  in Kernel module, 47
  initialize method and, 32
  initialize methods as, 32

method visibility, 31
  Module class and, 97
  Object class and, 47
private (Module), 98
private_class_method (Module), 97
private_instance_methods (Module), 97
private_methods (Kernel), 49
Proc class
  built-in library, 100
  completion_proc function and, 146
  proc function and, 42
  set_trace_func() function and, 43
  trace_var() function and, 46
Process module, 32, 89
profiler, 43, 169
--prompt option, 171
--prompt-mode option, 171
properties, classes and methods, 31
protected , 31, 49
protected (Module), 98
protected_instance_methods (Module), 97
protected_methods (Kernel), 49
protect_signal (PTY), 145
protocols (see specific protocol names)
prune (Find), 142
pseudo-variables, 16
PStore class, 153
PTY module, 145
public, 31, 49
public (Module), 98
public_class_method (Module), 97
public_instance_methods (Module), 97
public_methods (Kernel), 49
push
  Array, 63
  Queue, 150
putbinaryfile (Net::FTP), 119
putc
  IO, 77
  Kernel, 42
puts
  IO, 77
  Kernel, 43
pwd
  Dir, 88
  Net::FTP, 119

Q

Queue class, 150
quiet (GetoptLong), 144
quiet? (GetoptLong), 144

quit (Net::FTP), 120
quote (Regexp), 57
quotient, 70

R

-r option, 6, 34, 166, 170, 171
RAA (Ruby Application Archive), 174
radio_button (CGI), 132
radio_group (CGI), 132
raise, 29, 43, 92
rand function, 43
random numbers, 43, 44
Range class, 104
range operators, 18
RangeError class, 94
rank (Matrix), 156
rassoc (Array), 63
Rational class, 154, 155
Rational (Rational), 155
raw (Curses), 138
RCR (Ruby Change Requests), 179
rdev (File::Stat), 85
read
  Dir, 88
  IO, 77
readable?
  File, 81, 86
  File::Stat, 85
readable_real?
  File, 81
  File::Stat, 85
  FileTest, 86
readchar (IO), 77
readline, 37, 43, 77, 145
Readline module, 145, 146
--readline option, 171
readlines, 43, 75, 77
readlink (File), 81
ready (Net::SMTP), 127
real (Complex), 154
recv (BasicSocket), 112
recvfrom
  IPSocket, 112
  Socket, 117
  UNIXSocket, 115
redo statement, 27
refresh
  Curses, 138
  Curses::Window, 139
Regexp class, 57
RegexpError class, 94

regular? (Matrix), 157
rehash (Hash), 66
reject
   Array, 63
   Enumerable, 68
   Hash, 66
reject!
   Array, 63
   Hash, 66
remainder (Numeric), 70
remainders, 70
remove_const (Module), 98
remove_instance_variable (Kernel), 47
remove_method (Module), 98
rename
   File, 81
   Net::FTP, 120
   Net::IMAP, 123
reopen
   File, 82
   IO, 77
reorganize (GDBM), 152
repetition, characters expressing, 13
replace
   Array, 63
   Hash, 66
   String, 53
require, 34, 42, 43
rescue clause
   exception handling and, 28
   method definitions and, 22
   while statement and, 26
rescue statement, 28
reserved words, 9
reset (CGI), 132
reset_signal (PTY), 145
respond_to? (Kernel), 49
responses (Net::IMAP), 123
restore
   database manager, 136
   Marshal, 104
resume (Net::FTP), 120
retry statement, 28
return_code (Net::FTP), 120
reverse
   Array, 63
   String, 53
reverse!
   Array, 63
   String, 53

reverse_each (Array), 63
rewind
   Dir, 88
   IO, 78
RFC-1123 (date and time formatting), 130
RFC-1321 (MD5 class), 164
rfc1123_date(CGI), 130
ri (Ruby Interactive Reference), 173
rindex
   Array, 63
   String, 53
rjust (String), 53
rmdir
   Dir, 88
   File, 34
   Net::FTP, 120
rm_f (File), 143
root? (PStore), 153
round (Numeric0, 70
row (Matrix), 157
rows (Matrix), 155
row_size (Matrix), 157
row_vector (Matrix), 155
row_vectors (Matrix), 157
Ruby, 176–178
RUBYLIB (environment variable), 7, 34
RUBYLIB_PREFIX (environment
     variable), 7
ruby-mode for Emacs, 173
RUBYOPT (environment variable), 7, 34
RUBYPATH (environment variable), 7
RUBY_PLATFORM, 38
RUBY_RELEASE_DATE, 38
RUBYSHELL (environment variable), 8
RUBY_VERSION, 38
run (Thread), 92
RuntimeError, 29, 43, 94, 144

S

-S option, 7, 34
-s option, 6, 34, 173
s (conversion specifier), 44
$SAFE
   RUBYSHELL and, 7
   security and, 33
   taint mode and, 7
   variable, 6, 37
safe_level (Thread), 92
safe_unlink (File), 143

scalar (Matrix), 156
scan
  Kernel, 43
  String, 53
screens, 137, 138
ScriptError class, 94, 95
scrolling_list (CGI), 132
SDBM class, 152
search (Net::IMAP), 124
search paths, 7
sec (Time), 108
security, 3, 6, 33–35
SecurityError class, 94
seek
  Dir, 88
  IO, 78
select
  Enumerable, 68
  example, 2
  IO, 76
  Kernel, 43
  Net::IMAP, 124
self (pseudo-variable), 16
send
  BasicSocket, 112
  Kernel, 49
  UDPSocket, 113
send_mail (Net::SMTP), 127
sendmail (Net::SMTP), 127
separators, 5, 36
setgid?
  File, 81
  File::Stat, 85
  FileTest, 86
setgid, security checking, 33
setobj (SimpleDelegator), 158
set_options (GetoptLong), 144
setpgid
  Process, 90
  security level 2 and, 34
setpgrp (Process), 90
setpos
  Curses, 138
  Curses::Window, 139
setpriority
  Process, 90
  security level 2 and, 34
setsid
  Process, 90
  security level 2 and, 34
setsockopt (BasicSocket), 111

set_trace_func (Kernel), 43
setuid?
  File, 81
  File::Stat, 85
  FileTest, 86
setuid, security levels and, 33
sg (Date), 163
SHA1 class, 165
sha1 (SHA1), 165
SHELL, spawned processes and, 8
shift
  Array, 63
  Hash, 66
shutdown (BasicSocket), 111
signa (ConditionVariable), 148
signal handlers, trap() function and, 46
SimpleDelegator class, 158
--simple-prompt option, 172
sin (Math), 74
SingleForwardable module, 159
singleton classes, 30
singleton methods, 22, 49
Singleton module, 160
singleton_methods (Kernel), 49
singular? (Matrix), 157
size
  Array, 63
  File, 81
  File::Stat, 85
  FileTest, 86
  Hash, 66
  Integer, 71
  MatchData, 58
  Net::FTP, 120
  Net::POPMail, 126
  Queue, 150
  Range, 105
  String, 54
size?
  File, 81
  File::Stat, 85
  FileTest, 86
SizedQueue class, 150
SJIS (Shift-JIS), 6
sleep (Kernel), 44
slice
  Array, 64
  String, 54
slice!
  Array, 64
  String, 54

SMTP (Simple Mail Transfer
        Protocol), 126
Socket class, 111, 116, 117
socket?
    File, 81
    File::Stat, 85
    FileTest, 86
Socket::Constants module, 118
socketpair (Socket), 117
sort! (Array), 64
sort
    Array, 64
    Enumerable, 69
    Hash, 66
    Net::IMAP, 124
source (Regexp), 58
spaces
    as whitespace characters, 8
    completion_append_character and, 146
    directives and, 56, 63
    pretty() and, 130
spawn (PTY), 145
split
    File, 81
    Kernel, 44
    String, 54
sprintf function, 42, 44
sqrt (Math), 75
square? (Matrix), 157
squeeze (String), 54
squeeze! (String), 54
srand (Kernel), 35, 44
standard library, 110
StandardError class, 28, 94
standend
    Curses, 138
    Curses::Window, 139
standout
    Curses, 138
    Curses::Window, 139
start
    GC, 102
    Net::HTTP, 121
    Net::POP3, 125
    Net::SMTP, 127
    Thread, 92
stat
    File, 81
    IO, 78

status
    Net::FTP, 120
    Thread, 92
status (Net::IMAP), 124
STDERR, 37, 38
$stderr, 37, 38
STDIN, 6, 37, 39
$stdin, 37, 39
STDOUT, 37, 39
$stdout, 37, 39
stdscr (Curses), 138
step
    Date, 163
    Integer, 71
sticky?
    File, 81
    File::Stat, 85
    FileTest, 86
stop (Thread), 92
stop? (Thread), 92
store
    Hash, 67
    Net::IMAP, 124
strftime (Time), 108
String class, 10, 50–57
string
    Kernel, 45
    MatchData, 59
strings
    \A option and, 14
    concatenating, 10
    conversion specifiers and, 44
    converting, 55
    deleting, 51, 52, 54
    delimited, 11
    empty, 146
    length and, 54
    replacing, 52, 55
    source and, 58
    splitting contents, 54
    String class methods and, 50
    substitution in, 11
    types for new() class method, 147
    whitespace characters in, 8
strip (String), 54
strip! (String), 54
Struct class, 105

sub
  Kernel, 45
  String, 54
sub!
  Kernel, 45
  String, 54
subscribe (Net::IMAP), 124
substitution, command output to
      string, 11
subwin (Curses::Window), 139
succ
  Date, 162
  Integer, 72
  String, 53
succ! (String), 53
sum (String), 55
super statement, 24, 32
swapcase (String), 55
swapcase! (String), 55
Symbol class, 23
symlink (File), 81
symlink?
  File, 81
  File::Stat, 85
  FileTest, 86
sync (IO), 78
synchronize
  Monitor, 149
  Mutex, 149
--synopsis option, 173
syntax, 2, 5, 95
SyntaxError class, 95
syscall function, 34, 45
syscopy (File), 143
sysread (IO), 78
system
  Kernel, 45
  Net::FTP, 120
SystemCallError class, 95
SystemExit class, 95
SystemStackError class, 95
syswrite (IO), 78

T

-T option, 6, 33
t (Matrix), 157
taint (Kernel), 49
tainted code/data
  definition of, 33
  $SAFE and, 7, 37

security, 3, 33
  tainted method and, 49
tainted? (Kernel), 49
tan (Math), 75
TCP (Transmission Control Protocol), 113
TCPServer class, 114
TCPSocket class, 112–114
tel (IO), 77
tell
  Dir, 88
  IO, 78
telnet protocol, 127
telnetmode (Net::Telnet), 128
Tempfile class, 146
terminate (GetoptLong), 144
terminated? (GetoptLong), 144
ternary operator, 19
test, 34, 45
textarea (CGI), 132
text_field (CGI), 132
then (reserved word), 26, 28
Thomas, Dave, 173
Thread class, 91
ThreadGroup class, 93
threads
  built-in library, 91
  classes and, 148
  num_waiting instance method and, 150
  $SAFE in, 33
  security level 4 and, 35
  synchronizing, 148
  ThreadsWait instance, 151
ThreadsWait class, 151
throw function, 46
Time class, 106–109
time formatting, 130
timeout procedure, 43, 164
TimeoutError, 164
times
  Integer, 72
  Time, 106
to_a
  Enumerable, 68
  Hash, 67
  Kernel, 49
  MatchData, 59
today (Date), 162

to_f
    Integer, 72
    String, 55
    Time, 108
to_hash (Hash), 67
to_I (IO), 78
to_i
    IO, 76
    String, 55
    Time, 108
to_int (Integer), 72
to_io (IO), 78
top (Net::POPMail), 126
TOPLEVEL_BINDING, 39
to_proc (Method), 101
to_s (Kernel), 49
to_str (String), 55
tr
    Matrix, 157
    String, 55
tr! (String), 55
trace (Matrix), 157
tracer, 170, 171
Tracer library, 170
--tracer option, 172
trace_var function, 46
transaction (PStore), 153
transpose (Matrix), 157
trap, 34, 46
tr_s (String), 55
tr_s! (String), 55
TRUE constant, 38
true (pseudo-variable), 16
TrueClass class, 103
truncate
    File, 81, 82
    Numeric, 70
    security level 2 and, 34
try_enter (Monitor), 149
try_lock (Mutex), 150
try_mo_enter (MonitorMixin), 149
tty? (IO), 78
tv_sec (Time), 108
tv_usec (Time), 108
type (Kernel), 48
TypeError class, 95

U

u (conversion specifier), 44
UDP (User Data Protocol), 112
UDPSocket class, 113

uid
    File::Stat, 85
    Process, 89
uid_copy (Net::IMAP), 124
uid_fetch (Net::IMAP), 124
uid_search (Net::IMAP), 124
uid_sort (Net::IMAP), 124
uid_store (Net::IMAP), 125
umask (File), 34, 81
unbind (Method), 101
UnboundMethod, 101
undef statement, 24
undefine_finalizer (ObjectSpace0, 103
undef_method (Module), 99
unescape (CGI), 130
unescapeElement (CGI), 130
unescapeHTML (CGI), 130
ungetc (IO), 78
ungetch (Curses), 138
uniq (Array), 64
uniq! (Array), 64
unit (Matrix), 155
Unix domain, 115
UNIXServer class, 116
UNIXSocket class, 115
unless statement, 25
unlink
    Dir, 88
    File, 79
unlock (Mutex), 150
unpack String), 55
unshift (Array), 64
unsubscribe (Net::IMAP), 124
untaint (Kernel), 49
until statement, 26, 27
untrace_var (Kernel), 46
upcase (String), 57
upcase! (String), 57
update
    CGI::Session, 136
    database manager, 136
    Hash, 67
    MD5, 165
    SHA1, 165
uppercase characters
    capitalize and, 51
    constants and, 16
    downcase and, 52
    identifiers as, 9
    swapcase and, 55
    upcase and, 57

upto
  Date, 163
  Integer, 72
  String, 57
URL-encoding, 130
usec (Time), 108
UTC (Coordinated Universal Time), 119
utc (Time), 107, 109
utc? (Time), 109
UTF-8, 6, 178
utime (File), 81

V

-v option, 6, 37, 171, 173, 176
value? (Hash), 67
value (Thread), 93
values
  Hash, 67
  Struct, 106
variables
  environment, 7
  identifiers as, 9
  instance, 35
  predefined, 36–38
  reserved words and, 9
  symbols and, 12
  types of, 15–17
$VERBOSE (predefined variable), 37
verbose mode, 6
--verbose option, 6, 37
version, displaying, 6
--version option, 6, 171, 173
vi editor, 146
vi_editing_mode (Readline), 146

W

-w option, 6, 8, 15, 37
wait
  ConditionVariable, 148
  Process, 90
wait2 (Process), 90
waitfor (Net::Telnet), 129
waitpid (Process), 90
waitpid2 (Process), 90
wakeup (Thread), 93
wday
  Date, 163
  Time, 109
web sites
  current Ruby version, 176
  Ebb download, 174

eruby download, 174
RAA, 174
ri download, 173
Ruby, 1
Ruby bug database, 176
submitting RCRs, 179
useful libraries, 3
welcome (Net::FTP), 120
when clause, 26
while (reserved word), 26
while statement, 18, 26, 27
whitespace, 8, 12, 14, 54
width (flag), 44
Win32API class, 147
windows, 138, 147
WNOHANG constant, 90
writable?
  File, 81
  File::Stat, 85
  FileTest, 86
writable_real?
  File, 82
  File::Stat, 85
  FileTest, 87
write
  IO, 78
  Net::Telnet, 129
WUNTRACE constant, 90
WUNTRACED constant, 90

X

-X option, 6, 34
$-x variable, 37
-x option, 6, 14
X (conversion specifier), 44
x (conversion specifier), 44
XOR, TrueClass class and, 103

Y

-y option, 6
yday
  Date, 163
  Time, 109
year
  Date, 163
  Time, 109
yield statement, 24, 27
--yydebug option, 6

Z

zero (Matrix), 156
zero?
  File, 82
  File::Stat, 85
  FileTest, 87
  Numeric, 70
ZeroDivisionError class, 95
zone (Time), 109

About the Author

Yukihiro Matsumoto ("Matz"), the creator of Ruby, is a professional programmer who worked for the Japanese open source company, *netlab.jp*. Matz is also known as one of the open source evangelists in Japan. He's released several open source products, including cmail, the Emacs-based mail user agent, written entirely in Emacs Lisp. Ruby is his first piece of software that has become known outside of Japan.

Colophon

Our look is the result of reader comments, our own experimentation, and feedback from distribution channels. Distinctive covers complement our distinctive approach to technical topics, breathing personality and life into potentially dry subjects.

The animal on the cover of *Ruby in a Nutshell* is a wild goat. Also known as a bezoar goat (*Capra aegagrus*), this species, found on the Greek islands and in Turkey, Iran, Turkmenia, and Pakistan, can grow to 300 pounds and up to 4 feet tall.

Goats have cloven hooves, which means they are split into two toes. Both males and females have short beards the same color as their wool and horns that curve backward. Bezoar goat horns are scimitar-shaped with sharp inside edges, and their bodies are covered in a coarse wool that can be black, brown, gray, red, or white. Their wool helps them survive harsh climates. Bezoar goats are herbivores, and their diet consists of grass, twigs, leaves, berries, and bark. Wild female and baby goats live together in packs of about 50; males live by themselves or in all-male packs. During the mating season, males give off an oily substance from their skin that attracts females. Males can get into terrific fights over females, and the winning male gets to mate. Females give birth to one or two babies, or kids.

Wild goats are listed as vulnerable in the 1996 IUCN *Red List of Threatened Animals*. An animal is listed as vulnerable when it isn't critically endangered but faces a high risk of extinction in the wild. Bezoar goats are losing more and more land to development in their native countries.

Mary Anne Weeks Mayo was the production editor and proof reader, and Ellie Cutler was the copyeditor for *Ruby in a Nutshell*. Darren Kelly and Sheryl Avruch provided quality control. Derek DiMatteo provided production assistance. Lucie Haskins wrote the index.

Hanna Dyer designed the cover of this book, based on a series design by Edie Freedman. The cover image is a 19th-century engraving from the Dover Pictorial Archive. Emma Colby produced the cover layout with QuarkXPress 4.1 using Adobe's ITC Garamond font. Melanie Wang designed the interior layout based on a series design by Nancy Priest. Neil Walls converted the files from Microsoft Word to FrameMaker 5.5.6 using tools created by Mike Sierra. The text and heading fonts are ITC Garamond Light and Garamond Book. This colophon was compiled by Mary Anne Weeks Mayo

Whenever possible, our books use a durable and flexible lay-flat binding. If the page count exceeds this binding's limit, perfect binding is used.

More Titles from O'Reilly

Scripting Languages

Programming Python, 2nd Edition

By Mark Lutz
2nd Edition March 2001
1256 pages, Includes CD-ROM
ISBN 0-596-00085-5

Programming Python, 2nd Edition,
focuses on advanced applications of
Python, an increasingly popular
object-oriented scripting language.
Endorsed by Python creator Guido
van Rossum, it demonstrates advanced Python programming techniques, and addresses software design issues
such as reusability and object-oriented programming. The
enclosed platform-neutral CD-ROM has book examples
and various Python-related packages, including the full
Python Version 2.0 source code distribution.

Learning Python

By Mark Lutz & David Ascher
1st Edition April 1999
384 pages, ISBN 1-56592-464-9

Learning Python is an introduction
to the increasingly popular Python
programming language—an interpreted, interactive, object-oriented,
and portable scripting language. This
book thoroughly introduces the ele-
ments of Python: types, operators, statements, classes,
functions, modules, and exceptions. It also demonstrates
how to perform common programming tasks and write
real applications.

Python Programming on Win32

By Mark Hammond & Andy Robinson
1st Edition January 2000
674 pages, ISBN 1-56592-621-8

Despite Python's increasing popularity
on Windows, *Python Programming
on Win32* is the first book to demon-
strate how to use
it as a serious Windows development
and administration tool. This book
addresses all the basic technologies for common integra-
tion tasks on Windows, explaining both the Windows issues
and the Python code you need to glue things together.

Tcl/Tk Tools

By Mark Harrison
1st Edition September 1997
678 pages, Includes CD-ROM
ISBN 1-56592-218-2

One of the greatest strengths of Tcl/Tk
is the range of extensions written for
it. This book clearly documents the
most popular and robust extensions—by the people who created
them—and contains information on configuration,
debugging, and other important tasks. The CD-ROM
includes Tcl/Tk, the extensions, and other tools docu-
mented in the text both in source form and as binaries for
Solaris and Linux.

Exploring Expect

By Don Libes
1st Edition December 1994
602 pages, ISBN 1-56592-090-2

Written by the author of Expect, this is
the first book to explain how this part
of the Unix toolbox can be used to
automate Telnet, FTP, passwd, rlogin,
and hundreds of other interactive
applications. Based on Tcl (Tool
Command Language), Expect lets you automate interactive
applications that have previously been extremely difficult
to handle with any scripting language.

Tcl/Tk in a Nutshell

By Paul Raines & Jeff Tranter
1st Edition March 1999
456 pages, ISBN 1-56592-433-9

The Tcl language and Tk graphical
toolkit are powerful building blocks
for custom applications. This quick
reference briefly describes every command and option in the core Tcl/Tk
distribution, as well as the most popular extensions. Keep it on your desk
as you write scripts, and you'll be able to quickly find the
particular option you need.

Scripting Languages

Python & XML

By Christopher A. Jones & Fred Drake
1st Edition December 2001 (est.)
400 pages (est.), ISBN 0-596-00128-2

This book has two objectives: to provide a comprehensive reference on using XML with Python and to illustrate the practical applications of these technologies (often coupled with cross-platform tools) in an enterprise environment. Loaded with practical examples, it also shows how to use Python to create scalable XML connections between popular distributed applications such as databases and web servers. Covers XML flow analysis and details ways to transport XML through a network.

Python Standard Library

By Fredrik Lundh
1st Edition May 2001
300 pages, ISBN 0-596-00096-0

Python Standard Library, an essential guide for serious Python programmers, delivers accurate, author-tested documentation of all the modules in the Python Standard Library, along with over 300 annotated example scripts using the modules. This version of the book covers all the new modules and related information for Python 2.0, the first major release of Python in four years.

Tcl/Tk Pocket Reference

By Paul Raines
1st Edition October 1998
94 pages, ISBN 1-56592-498-3

A companion volume to *Tcl/Tk in a Nutshell*, the *Tcl/Tk Pocket Reference* is a handy reference guide to the basic Tcl language elements, Tcl and Tk commands, and Tk widgets. It provides easy access to just what you need and includes easy-to-understand summaries of Tcl/Tk language elements. Covers Tcl Version 8 and Tk Version 8.

PHP Pocket Reference

By Rasmus Lerdorf
1st Edition January 2000
120 pages, ISBN 1-56592-769-9

The *PHP Pocket Reference* is a handy quick reference for PHP, an open-source, HTML-embedded scripting language that can be used to develop web applications. This small book acts both as a perfect tutorial for learning the basics of PHP syntax and as a reference to the vast array of functions provided by PHP.

Python Pocket Reference, 2nd Edition

By Mark Lutz
2nd Edition December 2001 (est.)
128 pages (est.), ISBN 0-596-00189-4

This book is a companion volume to two O'Reilly animal guides: *Programming Python* and *Learning Python*. It summarizes Python statements and types, built-in functions, commonly used library modules, and other prominent Python language features.

O'REILLY®

TO ORDER: **800-998-9938** • **order@oreilly.com** • **www.oreilly.com**
ONLINE EDITIONS OF MOST O'REILLY TITLES ARE AVAILABLE BY SUBSCRIPTION AT **safari.oreilly.com**
ALSO AVAILABLE AT MOST RETAIL AND ONLINE BOOKSTORES

Linux

Using Samba

By Peter Kelly, Perry Donham
& David Collier-Brown
1st Edition November 1999
416 pages, Includes CD-ROM
ISBN 1-56592-449-5

Samba turns a Unix or Linux system
into a file and print server for
Microsoft Windows network clients.
This complete guide to Samba admin-
istration covers basic 2.0 configuration, security, logging,
and troubleshooting. Whether you're playing on one note
or a full three-octave range, this book will help you maintain an efficient and secure server. Includes a CD-ROM of
sources and ready-to-install binaries.

Managing & Using MySQL, 2nd Edition

By George Reese, Randy Jay Yarger
& Tim King
2nd Edition January 2002 (est.)
504 pages (est.), ISBN 0-596-00211-4

This edition retains the best features
of the first edition, while adding the
latest on MySQL and the relevant programming language interfaces, with
more complete reference informa-
tion. The administration section is greatly enhanced; the
programming language chapters have been updated—
especially the Perl and PHP chapters—and new additions
include chapters on security and extending MySQL and a
system tables reference.

Linux Network Administrator's Guide, 2nd Edition

By Olaf Kirch & Terry Dawson
2nd Edition June 2000
506 pages, ISBN 1-56592-400-2

Fully updated, this comprehensive,
impressive introduction to networking
on Linux now covers firewalls, including the use of ipchains and iptables
(netfilter), masquerading, and
accounting. Other new topics include
Novell (NCP/IPX) support and INN (news administration).
Original material on serial connections, UUCP, routing
and DNS, mail and News, SLIP and PPP, NFS, and NIS has
been thoroughly updated.

Understanding the Linux Kernel

By Daniel P. Bovet & Marco Cesati
1st Edition October 2000
650 pages, ISBN 0-596-00002-2

Understanding the Linux Kernel
helps readers understand how Linux
performs best and how it meets the
challenge of different environments.
The authors introduce each topic by
explaining its importance, and show
how kernel operations relate to the utilities that are familiar to Unix programmers and users.

UNIX Power Tools, 2nd Edition

By Jerry Peek, Tim O'Reilly
& Mike Loukides
2nd Edition August 1997
1120 pages, Includes CD-ROM
ISBN 1-56592-260-3

Loaded with practical advice about
almost every aspect of Unix, this second edition of UNIX Power Tools
addresses the technology that Unix
users face today. You'll find thorough coverage of POSIX
utilities, including GNU versions, detailed bash and tcsh
shell coverage, a strong emphasis on Perl, and a CD-ROM
that contains the best freeware available.

Linux Device Drivers, 2nd Edition

By Alessandro Rubini & Jonathan Corbet
2nd Edition June 2001
586 pages, ISBN 0-59600-008-1

This practical guide is for anyone who
wants to support computer peripher-
als under the Linux operating system.
It shows step-by-step how to write a
driver for character devices, block
devices, and network interfaces,
illustrating with examples you can compile and run. The
second edition covers Kernel 2.4 and adds discussions of
symmetric multiprocessing (SMP), Universal Serial Bus
(USB), and some new platforms.

How to stay in touch with O'Reilly

1. Visit Our Award-Winning Web Site

http://www.oreilly.com/

★ "Top 100 Sites on the Web" —PC Magazine
★ "Top 5% Web sites" —Point Communications
★ "3-Star site" —The McKinley Group

Our web site contains a library of comprehensive product information (including book excerpts and tables of contents), downloadable software, background articles, interviews with technology leaders, links to relevant sites, book cover art, and more. File us in your Bookmarks or Hotlist!

2. Join Our Email Mailing Lists

New Product Releases

To receive automatic email with brief descriptions of all new O'Reilly products as they are released, send email to:

ora-news-subscribe@lists.oreilly.com
Put the following information in the first line of your message (not in the Subject field):
subscribe ora-news

O'Reilly Events

If you'd also like us to send information about trade show events, special promotions, and other O'Reilly events, send email to:
ora-news-subscribe@lists.oreilly.com
Put the following information in the first line of your message (not in the Subject field):
subscribe ora-events

3. Get Examples from Our Books via FTP

There are two ways to access an archive of example files from our books:

Regular FTP

• ftp to:
ftp.oreilly.com
(login: anonymous
password: your email address)
• Point your web browser to:
ftp://ftp.oreilly.com/

FTPMAIL

• Send an email message to:
ftpmail@online.oreilly.com
(Write "help" in the message body)

4. Contact Us via Email

order@oreilly.com
To place a book or software order online. Good for North American and international customers.

subscriptions@oreilly.com
To place an order for any of our newsletters or periodicals.

books@oreilly.com
General questions about any of our books.

cs@oreilly.com
For answers to problems regarding your order or our products.

booktech@oreilly.com
For book content technical questions or corrections.

proposals@oreilly.com
To submit new book or software proposals to our editors and product managers.

international@oreilly.com
For information about our international distributors or translation queries. For a list of our distributors outside of North America check out:
http://www.oreilly.com/distributors.html

5. Work with Us

Check out our website for current employment opportunites:
http://jobs.oreilly.com/

O'Reilly & Associates, Inc.
1005 Gravenstein Hwy North
Sebastopol, CA 95472 USA
TEL 707-829-0515 or 800-998-9938
(6am to 5pm PST)
FAX 707-829-0104

Titles from O'Reilly

PROGRAMMING

C++: The Core Language
Practical C++ Programming
Practical C Programming,
  3rd Ed.
High Performance Computing,
  2nd Ed.
Programming Embedded Systems
  in C and C++
Mastering Algorithms in C
Advanced C++ Techniques
POSIX 4: Programming for the
  Real World
POSIX Programmer's Guide
Power Programming with RPC
UNIX Systems Programming
  for SVR4
Pthreads Programming
CVS Pocket Reference
Advanced Oracle PL/SQL
Oracle PL/SQL Guide to Oracle8i
  Features
Oracle PL/SQL Programming,
  2nd Ed.
Oracle Built-in Packages
Oracle PL/SQL Developer's
  Workbook
Oracle Web Applications
Oracle PL/SQL Language Pocket
  Reference
Oracle PL/SQL Built-ins Pocket
  Reference
Oracle SQL*Plus: The Definitive
  Guide
Oracle SQL*Plus Pocket Reference
Oracle Essentials
Oracle Database Administration
Oracle Internal Services
Oracle SAP
Guide to Writing DCE Applications
Understanding DCE
Visual Basic Shell Programming
VB/VBA in a Nutshell:
  The Language
Access Database Design
  & Programming, 2nd Ed.
Writing Word Macros
Applying RCS and SCCS
Checking C Programs with Lint
VB Controls in a Nutshell
Developing Asp Components,
  2nd Ed.
Learning WML & WMLScript
Writing Excel Macros
Windows 32 API Programming
  with Visual Basic
ADO: The Definitive Guide

USING THE INTERNET

Internet in a Nutshell
Smileys
Managing Mailing Lists

WEB

Apache: The Definitive Guide,
  2nd Ed.
Apache Pocket Reference
ASP in a Nutshell, 2nd Ed.
Cascading Style Sheets
Designing Web Audio
Designing with JavaScript,
  2nd Ed.
DocBook: The Definitive Guide
Dynamic HTML:
  The Definitive Reference
HTML Pocket Reference
Information Architecture
  for the WWW
JavaScript: The Definitive Guide,
  3rd Ed.
Java & XML, 2nd Ed.
JavaScript Application Cookbook
JavaScript Pocket Reference
Practical Internet Groupware
PHP Pocket Reference
Programming Coldfusion
Photoshop for the Web, 2nd Ed.
Web Design in a Nutshell, 2nd Ed.
Webmaster in a Nutshell, 2nd Ed.
Web Navigation: Designing the
  User Experience
Web Performance Tuning
Web Security & Commerce
Writing Apache Modules with
  Perl and C

UNIX

SCO UNIX in a Nutshell
Tcl/Tk in a Nutshell
The Unix CD Bookshelf, 2nd Ed.
UNIX in a Nutshell,
  System V Edition, 3rd Ed.
Learning the Unix Operating
  System, 4th Ed.
Learning vi, 6th Ed.
Learning the Korn Shell
Learning GNU Emacs, 2nd Ed.
Using csh & tcsh
Learning the bash Shell, 2nd Ed.
GNU Emacs Pocket Reference
Exploring Expect
Tcl/Tk Tools
Tcl/Tk in a Nutshell
Python Pocket Reference

USING WINDOWS

Windows Me: The Missing Manual
PC Hardware in a Nutshell
Optimizing Windows for Games,
  Graphics, and Multimedia
Outlook 2000 in a Nutshell
Word 2000 in a Nutshell
Excel 2000 in a Nutshell
Windows 2000 Pro:
  The Missing Manual

JAVA SERIES

Developing Java Beans
Creating Effective JavaHelp
Enterprise JavaBeans, 3rd Ed.
Java Cryptography
Java Distributed Computing
Java Enterprise in a Nutshell
Java Examples in a Nutshell,
  2nd Ed.
Java Foundation Classes
  in a Nutshell
Java in a Nutshell, 3rd Ed.
Java Internationalization
Java I/O
Java Native Methods
Java Network Programming,
  2nd Ed.
Java Performance Tuning
Java Security
Java Servlet Programming
Java ServerPages
Java Threads, 2nd Ed.
Jini in a Nutshell
Learning Java

GRAPHICS & MULTIMEDIA

MP3: The Definitive Guide
Director in a Nutshell
Lingo in a Nutshell

X WINDOW

Vol. 1: Xlib Programming Manual
Vol. 2: Xlib Reference Manual
Vol. 4M: X Toolkit Intrinsics
  Programming Manual,
  Motif Ed.
Vol. 5: X Toolkit Intrinsics
  Reference Manual
Vol. 6A: Motif Programming
  Manual
Vol. 6B: Motif Reference Manual,
  2nd Ed.

PERL

Advanced Perl Programming
CGI Programming with Perl,
  2nd Ed.
Learning Perl, 2nd Ed.
Learning Perl for Win32 Systems
Learning Perl/Tk
Mastering Algorithms with Perl
Mastering Regular Expressions
Perl Cookbook
Perl in a Nutshell
Programming Perl, 3rd Ed.
Perl CD Bookshelf
Perl Resource Kit – Win32 Ed.
Perl/Tk Pocket Reference
Perl 5 Pocket Reference,
  3rd Ed.

MAC

AppleScript in a Nutshell
AppleWorks 6:
  The Missing Manual
Crossing Platforms
iMovie: The Missing Manual
Mac OS in a Nutshell
Mac OS 9: The Missing Manual
REALbasic: The Definitive Guide

LINUX

Learning Red Hat Linux
Linux Device Drivers, 2nd Ed.
Linux Network Administrator's
  Guide, 2nd Ed.
Running Linux, 3rd Ed.
Linux in a Nutshell, 3rd Ed.
Linux Multimedia Guide

SYSTEM ADMINISTRATION

Practical UNIX & Internet Security,
  2nd Ed.
Building Internet Firewalls, 2nd Ed.
PGP: Pretty Good Privacy
SSH, The Secure Shell: The
  Definitive Guide
DNS and BIND, 3rd Ed.
The Networking CD Bookshelf
Virtual Private Networks, 2nd Ed.
TCP/IP Network Administration,
  2nd Ed.
sendmail Desktop Reference
Managing Usenet
Using & Managing PPP
Managing IP Networks
  with Cisco Routers
Networking Personal Computers
  with TCP/IP
Unix Backup & Recovery
Essential System Administration,
  2nd Ed.
Perl for System Administration
Managing NFS and NIS
Vol. 8: X Window System
  Administrator's Guide
Using Samba
UNIX Power Tools, 2nd Ed.
DNS on Windows NT
Windows NT TCP/IP Network
  Administration
DHCP for Windows 2000
Essential Windows NT System
  Administration
Managing Windows NT Logons
Managing the Windows 2000
  Registry

OTHER TITLES

PalmPilot: The Ultimate Guide,
  2nd Ed.
Palm Programming:
  The Developer's Guide

O'REILLY®

TO ORDER: 800-998-9938 • order@oreilly.com • www.oreilly.com
ONLINE EDITIONS OF MOST O'REILLY TITLES ARE AVAILABLE BY SUBSCRIPTION AT safari.oreilly.com
ALSO AVAILABLE AT MOST RETAIL AND ONLINE BOOKSTORES

International Distributors

http://international.oreilly.com/distributors.html • international@oreilly.com

UK, EUROPE, MIDDLE EAST, AND AFRICA (EXCEPT FRANCE, GERMANY, AUSTRIA, SWITZERLAND, LUXEMBOURG, AND LIECHTENSTEIN)

INQUIRIES
O'Reilly UK Limited
4 Castle Street
Farnham
Surrey, GU9 7HS
United Kingdom
Telephone: 44-1252-711776
Fax: 44-1252-734211
Email: information@oreilly.co.uk

ORDERS
Wiley Distribution Services Ltd.
1 Oldlands Way
Bognor Regis
West Sussex PO22 9SA
United Kingdom
Telephone: 44-1243-843294
UK Freephone: 0800-243207
Fax: 44-1243-843302 (Europe/EU orders)
or 44-1243-843274 (Middle East/Africa)
Email: cs-books@wiley.co.uk

FRANCE

INQUIRIES & ORDERS
Éditions O'Reilly
18 rue Séguier
75006 Paris, France
Tel: 33-1-40-51-71-89
Fax: 33-1-40-51-72-26
Email: france@oreilly.fr

GERMANY, SWITZERLAND, AUSTRIA, LUXEMBOURG, AND LIECHTENSTEIN

INQUIRIES & ORDERS
O'Reilly Verlag
Balthasarstr. 81
D-50670 Köln, Germany
Telephone: 49-221-973160-91
Fax: 49-221-973160-8
Email: anfragen@oreilly.de (inquiries)
Email: order@oreilly.de (orders)

CANADA

(FRENCH LANGUAGE BOOKS)
Les Éditions Flammarion ltée
375, Avenue Laurier Ouest
Montréal (Québec) H2V 2K3
Tel: 1-514-277-8807
Fax: 1-514-278-2085
Email: info@flammarion.qc.ca

HONG KONG

City Discount Subscription Service, Ltd.
Unit A, 6th Floor, Yan's Tower
27 Wong Chuk Hang Road
Aberdeen, Hong Kong
Tel: 852-2580-3539
Fax: 852-2580-6463
Email: citydis@ppn.com.hk

KOREA

Hanbit Media, Inc.
Chungmu Bldg. 210
Yonnam-dong 568-33
Mapo-gu
Seoul, Korea
Tel: 822-325-0397
Fax: 822-325-9697
Email: hant93@chollian.dacom.co.kr

PHILIPPINES

Global Publishing
G/F Benavides Garden
1186 Benavides Street
Manila, Philippines
Tel: 632-254-8949/632-252-2582
Fax: 632-734-5060/632-252-2733
Email: globalp@pacific.net.ph

TAIWAN

O'Reilly Taiwan
1st Floor, No. 21, Lane 295
Section 1, Fu-Shing South Road
Taipei, 106 Taiwan
Tel: 886-2-27099669
Fax: 886-2-27038802
Email: mori@oreilly.com

INDIA

Shroff Publishers & Distributors Pvt. Ltd.
12, "Roseland", 2nd Floor
180, Waterfield Road, Bandra (West)
Mumbai 400 050
Tel: 91-22-641-1800/643-9910
Fax: 91-22-643-2422
Email: spd@vsnl.com

CHINA

O'Reilly Beijing
SIGMA Building, Suite B809
No. 49 Zhichun Road
Haidian District
Beijing, China PR 100080
Tel: 86-10-8809-7475
Fax: 86-10-8809-7463
Email: beijing@oreilly.com

JAPAN

O'Reilly Japan, Inc.
Yotsuya Y's Building
7 Banch 6, Honshio-cho
Shinjuku-ku
Tokyo 160-0003 Japan
Tel: 81-3-3356-5227
Fax: 81-3-3356-5261
Email: japan@oreilly.com

SINGAPORE, INDONESIA, MALAYSIA, AND THAILAND

TransQuest Publishers Pte Ltd
30 Old Toh Tuck Road #05-02
Sembawang Kimtrans Logistics Centre
Singapore 597654
Tel: 65-4623112
Fax: 65-4625761
Email: wendiw@transquest.com.sg

AUSTRALIA

Woodslane Pty., Ltd.
7/5 Vuko Place
Warriewood NSW 2102
Australia
Tel: 61-2-9970-5111
Fax: 61-2-9970-5002
Email: info@woodslane.com.au

NEW ZEALAND

Woodslane New Zealand, Ltd.
21 Cooks Street (P.O. Box 575)
Waganui, New Zealand
Tel: 64-6-347-6543
Fax: 64-6-345-4840
Email: info@woodslane.com.au

ARGENTINA

Distribuidora Cuspide
Suipacha 764
1008 Buenos Aires
Argentina
Phone: 54-11-4322-8868
Fax: 54-11-4322-3456
Email: libros@cuspide.com

ALL OTHER COUNTRIES

O'Reilly & Associates, Inc.
1005 Gravenstein Hwy North,
Sebastopol, CA 95472 USA
Tel: 707-829-0515
Fax: 707-829-0104
Email: order@oreilly.com

O'REILLY®

TO ORDER: **800-998-9938** • **order@oreilly.com** • **www.oreilly.com**
ONLINE EDITIONS OF MOST O'REILLY TITLES ARE AVAILABLE BY SUBSCRIPTION AT **safari.oreilly.com**
ALSO AVAILABLE AT MOST RETAIL AND ONLINE BOOKSTORES